# KRISHNA

# KRISHNA

## A STUDY IN THE THEORY OF AVATARAS

By

**BHAGAVAN DAS**

GYAN

*Published by*

Gyan Publishing House
5, Ansari Road
Daryaganj, New Delhi-110002
Phone: 011-47034999, 9811692060
E-mail: books@gyanbooks.com

*Distribution Network*
gyanbooks.com
India, USA, Canada, UK, Australia



ISBN: 978-93-6208-069-1 (PB)
First Published, 1924

2nd Impression 2024

*Printed at:* Gyan Press, Delhi.



**KRISHNA**
Author: BHAGAVAN DAS

# KRISHNA

## A Study in the Theory of Avataras

"Bharat Ratna"
Dr. Bhagavan Das.
(7th Septr. 1955, on which date I received the medal from the hands of Rashtrapati Dr. Rajendra Prasad in N. Delhi).

# KRISHNA

## A STUDY IN THE THEORY OF AVATARAS

BY

**BHAGAVAN DAS**

1962

BHARATIYA VIDYA BHAVAN

CHAUPATTY : BOMBAY

## CONTENTS

# KRISHNA

## A STUDY IN THE THEORY OF AVATARAS

### THE TIME AND THE MAN

A WESTERN writer summing up the great qualities of Charlemagne, says that " he takes rank among the extraordinary men who, from time to time, appear to change the face of the world, and to inaugurate a new era in the destinies of mankind"; for Charlemagne, crowned first Emperor of the new Holy Roman Empire by Pope Leo III on Christmas Day in A.D. 800, completes the transition of Europe from the Dark Ages, which followed upon the break-up of the old Roman Empire, into the Middle Ages proper. The writer was evidently a believer in what has been called the School of Heroic History, the school which believes that the Great Man is the " ulitmate, inexplicable ground for understanding what happened in his day," or even that the history of a nation is only the sum of the adventurous biographies[1] of its Great Men. There has been much disputation whether the man makes the time or the time makes the man. The dispute is not new. It occurs in the *Maha-bharata*, as almost every

[1] Emerson thought : " There is properly no history. only biography."

large and important human problem does, together with its express or implied solution. The solution of this particular problem there given seems to support entirely the Heroic School. Bhishma says to Yudhishthira :

कालो वा कारणं राज्ञो राजा वा कालकारणम् ।
इति ते संशयो माभूद् राजा कालस्य कारणम् ॥

" Is the time the cause of the king, or is the king the cause of the time ? Let no such doubts trouble thee. The king makes the time."[2]

But while this was undoubtedly the appropriate answer in the immediate context, it should not be understood as wholly without reservations. While the modern Heroic School of History regards the Great Man as "inexplicable," the Purana School does not regard him as such. And this makes the great difference of significance of the same words, when uttered by the two different thinkers.

कृतं त्रेतायुगं चैव द्वापरं कलिरेव च ।
राज्ञो वृत्तानि सर्वाणि राजा हि युगमुच्यते ॥
कलि: प्रसुप्तो भवति स जाग्रद्द्वापरं युगं ।
कर्मस्वभ्युद्यतस्त्रेता विचरंस्तु कृतं युगं ॥ M.,ix,301-2

" The sovereign, the chief, the leader, induces high or low conduct in the people by his own example and precept. Thus is he the maker of

---

[2]The *Shukra-Niti*, a work on the art of government, and *Manu* have some more explicit verses,

आचारप्रेरको राजा ह्येतत् कालस्य कारणम् ।
यदि काल: प्रमाणं हि कस्माद्धर्मोऽस्ति कर्तृषु ॥ *S. N.* i., 22

the time. Slothful and vicious, he makes Kali ; wakeful and watchful, Dvapara ; attentive to duties, Treta ; spreading beneficence around actively, Satya-yuga." But it is also true that every people gets the government it deserves. It is a circle no doubt, but a " virtuous " circle, metaphysically, and not " vicious, " as the text should make clear. In Arabian Sufism, *abu-'l-waqt* is " the father of the time ", and *ibn-ul-waqt* " the son of the time." In other words, " the maker of a time, the creator of conditions, the epoch-maker," and " the child of his age, the creature of circumstances, the product of the period ". In Samskrt phrase, some *jivas* are *yuga-karaka, yuga-janaka, yuga-pravartaka,* others are *yuga-karita, yuga-janita, yuga-prerita.*

## The Theory of Avataras

The Purana School has a theory of its own as to these Great Men. They do not appear accidentally. They evolve from smallness to greatness, life after life, in accordance with laws. They are of various grades and kinds and degrees of power. They appear for special reasons in special circumstances. And this theory of Great Men is, as might be expected, part and parcel of the total Puranic theory of the nature of the Universe, and of the birth, the evolution, and the dissolution of world-systems therein. In other words, Great Men are part of a Great World-Plan, actors in a vast and complicated Drama, elaborately and minutely thought out by Supra-Consciousness.

As has been remarked in the West, " sciences are not many; Science is one." All the so-called separate sciences are but the shoots and branches of one main Root-Science, the Science of the Infinite Spirit, *Brahma-vidya*, the Science of the Self, *Atma-vidya*. Even so, varying the phrase, "religions may be many, but Religion is one". And the Religion of the Infinite Spirit or Consciousness is the same as the Science thereof. It is metaphysic and psychology in the fullest and most comprehensive sense; it includes the principles of super-physics as well as physics ; in it science and religion become one, *Vaidika Dharma*, "the Law and Religion of Knowledge," "Scientific Religion." While the *Darshana-sutras*[3] expound this *Atma-vidya* in an abstract form, the Puranas and Itihasas illustrate its principles concretely. In so doing they reconcile all conflicts of opinions by assigning to each view its proper time, place, and limits. There can be no more and no less conflict, as well as agreement, between the various sciences and views, than there is between the various features and aspects of Nature, the Nature of the Spirit, with which they severally and specially, *i.e.*, predominantly, deal and whose interdependence and organic unity they are all beginning again to recognise.

In this way we find, in the Puranas, both views under discussion duly reconciled by explanation of what the sense is, in which the man makes the time, and what that is, in which the time makes, or, better, brings the man. Time as *Kala* or *Maha-Kala*, the "moving" Spirit, the

---

[3]*Darshana-sutras*, the Aphorisms of the different systems of philosophy. Literally, *darshana* means *vision*, out-*look* upon life and upon the world, as well as *in*-look, *insight*, into the heart of things, into fundamental truth and reality. *Purana-Itihasa*, taken as one, means "ancient history," or, rather, "(the) permanent (principles, outlines and typical events. of all) history". It is to *Darshana* as concrete to abstract, as practice to theory, as particular illustration to general rule. Taken separately, the two words may be translated as Cosmology and Anthropology, broadly. It is significant that the first two volumes of Madame Blavatsky's *The Secret Doctrine* are respectively named Cosmogenesis and Anthropogenesis. They are new "editions" or versions of the old Purana and Itihasa, according to the requirements of the new times.

Great Mover, is but another name or aspect of the Oversoul whose sub-conscious, supra-conscious, or un-conscious Will-and-Imagination is the deep-lying cause of all the drama and panorama of all history, of all the world-process, and so brings into the play the so-called Great Man also, on the proper occasion.[4] Time as a particular era, of peace

---

[4]The word *Kala* means ordinarily what is understood by the word time ; but its etymology is, *kalayati iti Kalah,* that which *moves* all things. It has to be remembered that it is the Self, illusorily attaching itself to and then detaching itself from not-selves, which creates, gives rise to the mythical appearance of Time, Space, and Motion. (See *The Science of Peace*).

Will-and-Imagination is Kama-and-Sankalpa. Thus.

धर्ममूलोऽर्थ इत्युक्तः कामोऽर्थफलमुच्यते ।
संकल्पमूलास्ते सर्वे संकल्पो विषयात्मकः ॥

*Maha-bharata, Shanti,* ch.123.

सनातनो हि संकल्पः काम इत्यभिधीयते ।
संकल्पाभिरुचिः कामः सनातनतमोऽभवत् ॥
जगत्पतिरनिर्देश्यः सर्वगः सर्वभावनः ।
हृच्छयः सर्वभूतानां ज्येष्ठो रुद्रादपि प्रभुः ॥

*Maha-bharata, Anushasana,* ch. 131.

कामः सर्वमयः पुंसां स्वसंकल्पसमुद्भवः ।
कामात् सर्वे प्रवर्त्तंते लीयंते वृद्धिमागताः ॥

*Shiva Purana, Dharma Samhita,* ch. 8.

ध्यायतो विषयान् पुंसः संगस्तेषूपजायते ।
संगात् संजायते कामः कामात् क्रोधोऽभिजायते ॥ *Gita.*

" Dharma, lawful conduct. brings Artha. wealth, whence Kama, desire-fulfilment. All three are rooted in Sankalpa, Will-Ideation. It is the same as Kama, the Ancient. the Creator and Lord of all creatures, the Dweller in the heart of all things and beings, older than even

and goodwill, or of sin and sorrow, or of war between the opposite forces, is the effect of the working of a good great man or an evil great man or of sets of both the kinds working simultaneously ; for there are rogue-heroes as well as angel-heroes in the play; and in them appear in concentrated form the prevailing good and evil tendencies of the age.

In fact, the great Jaina writers, whose versions of the *Ramayana* and the *Mahabharata* are more "rationalistic," have a very illuminative theory that the avataras always come in opposed pairs, as *Narayana* and *Prati-Narayana*, the former representing the Good Force and the latter the Evil, as Rama and Ravana ; and history is fullest and vividest when the two forces, of love and of hate, are battling most strongly. Each requires the other, for its own *swarupa-siddhi*, self-expression, self-manifestation. And the more intense the opposition of the two, the more clear the definition of each. Gods and Titans, Angels and Devils, need each other ; and whenever the primal Energy awakens from sleep, it necessarily appears in both forms, Good as well as Evil, pain as well as pleasure. Briefly, Time as the Over-soul makes the man, time as an era is made by the man.

It may be mentioned here that the Puranas first sketch in very broad outlines the story of what, in modern terms, may be called (1) inorganic evolution ; then they describe (2) organic evolution in our little world-system, also in broad outlines ; then they set forth in a little more detail the aeonian unfoldment of the potencies of (3) the Human Race and of its (4) many sub-races ; and finally they describe in brief (5) the process of dissolution of a world-system.

---

Rudra-Anger. From Kama-Eros arise, and into It re-merge, all things. Imagination, attachment, love, hate, arise out of one another."

सर्गश्च प्रतिसर्गश्च वंशो मन्वंतराणि च ।
वंशानुचरितं चैव पुराणं पंचलक्षणम् ॥

"The Purana has five principal features" (as above).

In this way they perform the work of all the various schools of history now current, the date and fact school, the heroic, the sociological or anthropological or democratic, the naturalistic or materialistic or environmental, the idealistic, etc.[5] In connection with the story of the Human Kingdom mainly, and incidentally with that of the animal and the deva kingdoms, we find mention of the *Avataras*, the Great Men or Souls in the highest degree. They may, in a sense, be regarded as the very special and focussed manifestations of the *Sutr-atma*, the Thread-Soul, the Net-Soul, the Web-Soul, the Over-Soul, of the Human Race. Otherwise, indeed, the notion is familiar to the Indian that the One Life manifests in *all* creatures and not only in the remarkably great.

---

[5]See C. Delisle Burns's *Political Ideals*, ch. 1; (1) The business of history is simply to record events and their dates; (2) history is the record of the adventures of great men ; (3) the "people" of the past are the explanation of the "people" of to-day ; (4) natural causes, environment country, climate, race, physical products, supply and demand. bring about and explain history ; (5) the ideals of men mould history ; etc.

Tolstoy, in the last part of his famous novel, *War and Peace*, moved by righteous indignation against Napoleon for his wanton invasion of Russia, makes a minute and excellently reasoned examination of the claims of "heroes" and "geniuses" and their alleged "power" to make history. He comes to the conclusion, strictly accurate metaphysically, that all "power" is only in the Eternal, "in last analysis we reach the circle of Eternity"; and that "heroes" and "geniuses" have no free-will, but are only figure-heads and puppets in the hands of a divinely pre-ordained Destiny, and have no good reason at all for self-conceit. He adds : "We know not why there are wars and revolutions." Now Vedanta and

We read in the *Bhagavad-Gita :*

न तदस्ति विना यत्स्यान् मया भूतं चराचरम् । and
विष्टभ्याहमिदं कृत्स्नमेकांशेन स्थितो जगत् ।। and again,
यद् यद् विभूतिमत्सत्त्वं श्रीमदूर्जितमेव वा ।
तत्तदेवावगच्छ त्वं मम तेजोंशसंभवम् ।।

"While (the) I prevade (s) all things and all beings, moving and unmoving, yet extraordinarily splendid manifestations embody My (the I's) *tejas*-attribute, 'fire,' *active* Energy, in a special degree."

As there will not be occasion to refer to them again, a word may be given to the non-human (or sub or super human) avataras here. The Fish, Turtle, Boar, Man-Lion and Dwarf Incarnations of Vishnu may, in one sense, be regarded as Puranic allegories of the stages of psycho-

---

Purana give us some idea of a World-Plan, a Perpetual Drama, of the Spirit's descent into and reascent out of Matter, in pseudo-infinite ways, and thus help to explain why's. Incidentally they make clear that while all the dramatis personae are equally puppets in, and moved by, the Mind of the One Author, yet, as compared with each other, between themselves, some are "great" and "very great", and others "little" and "very little". After all, the words "great" and "little" must have their place, and their appropriate meaning too in the Play ! The sun is a sun, the candle is a candle ; though, of course, the sun has no right to be conceited, for the candle can light the poor man's cottage at night as the sun cannot ! Because all finites bear the same ratio to the Infinite, metaphysically, it does not follow that they are all equal to one another, empirically. Metaphysically, they have to be equal too. and therefore, the provision is made that all actors must play all parts, be suns as well as candles, turn by turn, over and over again, perpetually. (*Gita*, XV, 17; XVIII, 61; X, 41).

physical evolution, aquatic, reptilian, mammal,[6] lion, anthropoid and human. In another sense, they may be regarded as typifying the fact of the appearance of abnormal leaders amongst animals also ; Kipling's story of *The White Seal* and Thompson Seton's account of *Krag, the Kootenay Ram*, illustrate the same fact, in very modern language. A manifestation of *Shakti* (Cosmic Energy) in the shape of clouds of wasps for the destruction of an *Asura* (Titan) named Aruna, is mentioned in *Durga-sapta-shati*, and reminds one of the Egyptian plagues of flies, locusts, frogs, etc. Some avataras in the deva kingdom are mentioned in the Puranas, the deva kingdom and the human kingdom being, according to them, interdependent in various ways. But the human are obviously of most interest to us.

### THE OVERSOUL

Some of us may perhaps wonder : What is this Oversoul and what can be meant by its special manifestations ? The words of the *Gita*, we may say, sound impressive enough, but they do not come home to us.

Well, let us try to explain. We know that explaining is reducing the unfamiliar into terms of the familiar—nothing more. Let us do this in the present case.

There is vitality in all my body. But if I rest quietly, I do not feel it more keenly in any one

---

[6] सुरेष्वृषिष्वीश तथैव नृष्वपि तिर्यक्षु यादःस्वपि तेऽजनस्य ।
जन्माऽसतां दुर्मदनिग्रहाय प्रभो विधातः सदनुग्रहाय च ॥

*Bhagavata*, X, xiv, 20. "O Birthless Lord of All, thy births among the gods, the rshis, men, animals, and ocean forms, are all intended for the one purpose of punishing the wicked and fostering the good."

part than in any other. Let a mosquito sting me, however, on the left hand. At once there is a concentration of feeling there ; and at the same time, there is another concentration of life-force in the other hand which rapidly moves over to brush off the mosquito and rub the smarting spot and restore equanimity there; this takes place even during sleep, sub-consciously or semi-consciously. This is possible because, while the two hands are separate, they are also bound in an organic unity. So foul secretions are counteracted by healthy secretions, or disease-microbes by phagocytes, in the same living organism. So, in a condition of ordinary peace and good government, if there is any special manifestation of lawlessness in any place, there is a special strengthening and concentration of the forces of lawfulness there, to counteract it. This is possible only because while the individual law-breakers and law-preservers are separate, they have also an underlying communal unity, like erring sin-causing passion and pricking conscience in the same human being.[7] This unity may not be visible to the physical eye, as in the other case, but it is as much a fact. Every one of us is constantly using the two words " I " and " We ". When he says " I," he is thinking of, or feeling, his individual soul ; when he says " We ", he is thinking of, or feeling, his Oversoul, the Communal Soul, the *Sutratma.*

But, someone may say, " We " is only a collection of " I's". Is it ? No; it is much more. It is the *principle* which collects and holds them together. It is that im-

---

[7]The *ashuddham-manas* or *ashubha-vasana,* and *shuddham-manas* or *shubha vasana* of Samskrt-Vedanta ; and the *nafas-ul-ammara* and *nafas-ul-lawwama* of Arabian Sufism.

palpable, invisible, yet very insistent *something* which makes them think and feel and act alike, for a common purpose, *which makes the collection possible.* If the simple little word "We" has any meaning, then the word "Oversoul" has also a meaning. In hunting diligently for the significance of the one, we will find the secret of the other ; as, should we but search diligently enough for the real meaning of that almost simpler word "I," we may find the utterly finite and infinitesimal as well as the Infinite itself. The modern expressions, "public opinion," "diffused intelligence," "collective mind," "mass-mind," "public spirit," "solidarity of man," "national enthusiasm," "general panic," "popular sentiment," etc., all indicate the presence and working of the same principle, the Oversoul or Group-soul.

मनो महान् मतिर्ब्रह्मा पूर्बुद्धिः ख्यातिरीश्वरः ।
प्रज्ञा चितिः स्मृतिः संविद् विपुरं चोच्यते बुधैः। ।
विद्यते स च सर्वस्मिन् सर्वं तस्मिश्च विद्यते ।
तस्मात्संविदिति प्रोक्तो महान् वै बुद्धिमत्तरैः ॥

*Vayu Purana,* I, iv.

"This Mahan (Mahat or Buddhi of the Sankhya), the Principle of Universal Intelligence, Cosmic Consciousness (Sub-or Supra-Consciousness) which exists in all things and in which all things exist, which is therefore known as *Sam-vit,*—this Principle has many names, Manas, Mati, Brahma, Puh, Khyati, Ishvara, Prajna, Chit, Smrti, Vipura, etc."[8]

---

[8]Arabian Sufism calls this Mahat-Buddhi by the name of *Aql-i-kul,* which also literally means the Universal Mind; also *Haqiqat-i-Muhammadi,* the Praiseworthy Truth.

This Buddhi, all-including Supra-conscious Wisdom, is said to be " the seed-store, the Principle, in the Nature of the Self, from which all avataras come ".

सर्वेषामवताराणां निधानं बीजमव्ययम् ॥

*Bhagavata*, I, iii,5.

In this Spiritual Intelligence or Pure Reason, which, in the general sense, constitutes the scheme of the whole world-process, are bound together the Atma and the Manas, the " I " and the " this ", the Infinite and the finite, the Universal and the individual, the Pratyag-atma, and the jiv-atma. This Buddhi (the Theosophist's sixth principle) is the nexus-maker and mediator (the Sufi's *barzakh*) between the Atma and the Manas (the seventh and fifth principles). In the particular sense, it is the plane of the vast hosts of the individual jivan-muktas, or rather videha-muktas, sons of God, holy ghosts and Christs, *arwah-i-qudsi* (or —*kamil* or— *rasidah*) who have succeeded in establishing connection, by having attained the enlightened reason, the illumined mind (*i.e.*, the sixth principle), between their individual mind or self and the Universal Self (*i.e.*, their fifth principle and the Universal Seventh) ; who are full of the Wisdom which sees both the Infinite and the finite, who have become possessed of special powers in consequence ; and who are, therefore, worthy and able to act as " mediators " between " God " and "man," the Universal and the individual, able to lead the latter to the former by gradual enlightenment of his mind, able to serve as Messengers, Prophets, Messiahs, Avataras, etc. They help to tie the " finite " soul to the Infinite and Immortal, and enable it " to cross the abyss," " to become safe," " emancipated," " free (of doubt and fear)"—in the general ense, as well as the technical one of special " initiations " (*diksha*).

### Its Manifestations

The law governing the extraordinary manifestations of the Oversoul is, according to the Puranas, the same as in the familiar case mentioned above. The law of analogy holds good here as elsewhere.

यदा यदा हि धर्मस्य ग्लानिर्भवति भारत ।
अभ्युत्थानमधर्मस्य तदात्मानं सृजाम्यहम् ॥
परित्राणाय साधूनां विनाशाय च दुष्कृताम् ।
धर्मसंस्थापनार्थाय संभवामि युगे युगे ॥ *Gita*, iv, 7-8

" For the advancement of ' civilising conventions and customs,' the institution of ' law and order,' the *re*-establishment of an old law and order, or it may be, the new establishment of a new law and order, for fostering the good and weeding out the evil—for this purpose, whenever the general forces of inertia, ignorance, sloth, vice and crime begin to prevail overmuch over the forces of virtue, love and goodness—the Self, the Universal I, appears as and in and through the Great Man, cycle after cycle, to re-establish the disturbed balance, in various ways." And

इत्थं यदा यदा बाधा दानवोत्था भविष्यति ।
तदा तदावतीर्याहं करिष्याम्यरिसंक्षयम् ॥

*Durga-sapta-shati.*

" Whenever the *danavas*, evil men, proceed to excess, (the) I will ' come down ' and destroy them."

### Religion and Civilisation

The birth and growth of every new civilisation, every new culture, have been preceded by a religion, re-*legere*, a re-binding together, anew, of human hearts, by a fresh faith, because civilisation, peace, progress, prosperity, are not possible without co-operation ; because co-operation is not possible without the binding together of human hearts ; and because that, again, is not possible without a common faith. But every fresh faith is only the refreshing of the one eternal faith in the Supreme and yet the nearest Object of faith, our own inmost *Self*, the God *in* us *all*. This ultimate and the other chief penultimate objects of faith, *viz.*, Life Immortal, the distinction between Love and Hate, Right and Wrong, Reward and Punishment, " As we sow, so must we reap"—these are the most ancient yet ever new, the most commonplace yet ever the most noble and most elevating, the most hackneyed yet ever the most vitally important, fundamentals of life and faith, in every special creed or code of life. Without the holy authority of these, the most impressive-seeming and pompously worded laws are mere suicidal cunning. This refreshened faith, harking back to these origins and foundations of all life, has therefore always come as *faith with reason* (or, indeed, with direct perception or intuition, the basis of reason), which is science (in contradistinction from faith without reason, which is superstition). Who, if he but have turned his mind's eye inward, has ever doubted, who can ever doubt, the existence of him-Self ? And this renewed faith in the Self has always brought in its train a new era of prosperity. Witness the Buddhist, the Christian, and the Islamic religions and corresponding cultures or civilisations and kingdoms. The rise of sects and even sub-sects within the fold of a major religion, has also given rise to important variations in the culture ; Protestantism, Quakerism, Mormonism, Chaitanyism, Sikhism, Jainism, Hina-yanism, Maha-yanism, Wahabism, Bahaism, are instances.

So the degeneration, decay and death of every old civilisation have been preceded by the corruption, decay and death of the religion (and therefore morals) which gave it being, and nursed and supported it in its growth and its prime—the death of the faith, namely, of human beings in the Eternal Principles, and in each other, primarily, and secondarily, an excessive clinging to the outer forms, rites and ceremonies and sacraments and conventions, which merely symbolised these Principles for that community; a clinging to the letter which killeth and a neglect of the Spirit which giveth life ; whence the break-down of sympathy and self-denying co-operation, and the uprush of all kinds of jealousies, selfishnesses, hatreds and conflicts, and the disruption of social solidarity, strength, and civilisation.

Therefore the Scriptures say, in various ways, that when virtue decays, and vice flourishes, *i.e.*, when the inner heart-faith in the one Self and the essential religion of all-embracing love weaken, and the outer forms, formalisms, narrow bigotries, and vicious practices and sectarianisms miscalled religion, which divide man from his brother man, strengthen, then the God in man, the Oversoul of Humanity, for its own self-preservation against the Demons of Mutual Hate and Internecine War, evolves new forces which simply *revive* that deep heart-faith, always *essentially* the same, though embodying itself in varying *forms*, from time to time.

## DAITYAS, DANAVAS, ETC.

It should be borne in mind that the Devas or Suras, and the Daityas, Danavas, Asuras, Rakshasas, etc., are all " cousins " or even " step-brothers, " in the poetic and allegorical language of the Puranas ; that, historically, they very probably mean different races and sub-races of the human race; that superphysically or psychically, they mean the same groups of *jivas* (souls) born in different races, at different times, now in a preponderantly selfish mood and now in an unselfish ; and that even "mystically," as Rama and Krishna are avataras of Vishnu, so Ravana and Kumbhakarna, Kamsa and Shishupala, etc., are avataras of Vishnu's *parshadas* or angel-attendants, are "fallen angels"—in the sense of fallen into evil ways as also into fleshly incarnations.

The *Bhagavata* expressly says that both the good and the evil forms are forms of the One Life.

स्वशांतरूपेष्वितरैः स्वरूपैरभ्यर्द्यमानेष्वनुकंपितात्मा ।
परावरेशो महदंशयुक्तो ह्यजोऽपि जातो भगवान्यथाग्निः ॥

III, ii, 15.

"Beholding His peaceful forms being oppressed by His own other restless embodiments, the compassioning Lord manifested Himself in a special body endowed with an extra-ordinary measure of the substance and quality of *Mahat* (the Uhiversal Mind), to restore the due balance and proportion between the two, even as the ever-present but latent *agni*-fire flames up and appears to be born out of combustibles under friction or violent impact."

Another and less known interpretation of the verse, "When the forces of evil begin to prevail, etc.," may be mentioned here, as of importance for the philosophical understanding of world-events. While avataras adjust the good and bad karma of others, they, incidentally, *expiate their own evil karma* at the same time, by their own voluntary sufferings in the course of those adjustments. The *shapa-s*, "curses," "dooms," laid upon the high *devas*, "gods", mostly by the *rshis*, "saints and sages," in accordance with which these "gods" take birth on earth as greater or lesser avataras, require to be pondered upon, in this reference. They are impartially mentioned by the same Puranas which describe the glories of these avataras. The nature of the errors for which these dooms are pronounced ; the nature of these pronouncements, whether they have a compelling force or are merely declarations of conseqences ; the results of them to the *rshis* themselves ; the nature of the gods, whether they are predominantly personal, or are predominantly impersonal nature-forces, etc.—all these are connected and interesting questions for investigation, the answers to which may be found in the same Puranas also.

It may also be called to mind here that if the avataras of good expiate their previous sins in this way, the avataras of evil expiate or exhaust by their later self-willed and vicious indulgences their previous virtues and the stores of merit they had accumulated by severe asceticism. The "ten-headed" Ravana, symbol of his excessively intellectual nation, won his "golden" city of Lanka (formerly belonging to Kubera, the god of wealth) after conquering the "gods," by the sacrifice of his own "heads" over and over again, in the course of the *tapas*-striving of "thousands of years". Even so the present excessively "intellectual" nations of the West have conquered the gods of earth, water, fire, air, and electricity, and won the stores of Mammon and Bacchus, by the sacrifice and death, in the course of centuries, of their many "heads," their best and most courageous, enterprising and adventurous explorers, scientific experimenters, aviators, submarinists, electricians, engineers, soldiers, merchants and sailors ; and are now indulging themselves in inordinate luxuries, for which the " exploitation " of vast masses of weaker peoples is indispensable ; and are thus preparing the way for their own downfall—through repeated internecine wars apparently, as in the case of the Titan brothers Sunda and Upa-sunda.[9]

## MAIN KINDS OF GREAT MEN

Obviously, there are many kinds and grades of *dharma*, of " law and order ". Therefore there are as many kinds and grades of promoters and protectors thereof. The main kinds are three. The functions of life and mind are three : knowing, desiring, acting. Therefore the essential business of all true law and order is to promote right knowledge, right desire, and right action.

When this is done, everything is done. Law and order, Dharma, does not mean the theocrat's conception of it ; it does not mean what any particular pope or priest thinks, for his own and his class's and caste's aggrandisement, should be the law and order; or what any autocrat, aristocrat, bureaucrat thinks it ought to be ; or any plutocrat ; or any

[9]Sunda and Upa-sunda vowed and vigilled and fasted for hundreds of years. Brahma appeared and said : " Ask what you want." " Immortality." " Impossible ; but you can choose your own manner of death." " All right." They consulted together : " Let us trick the Ancient Personage ; let us say we will not be killed except by each other ; we love each other, so it is obvious that will never be ; and we shall be immortal after all." They stated their choice to Brahma. "Very good." Then the two had their good time ; and the rest of the world its bad time. The gods grew sick. They went and wailed before the Ancient Universal Mind. And the Mind pondered, and gathered all the elements of beauty, from everything that was beautiful, " sesamum-seed by sesamum-seed ", grain by grain. And with that heap of beauty He fashioned Til-ot-tama, the most beautiful nymph of heaven created up to then. She

particular democrat, for the matter of that. The ancient conception of Dharma is that it is that Code of Life which establishes a due balance and proportion between all these four fundamental and true "estates of the realm," *viz.*, the clergy or the wise and the learned, the nobles or the office-bearers and the soldiers, the merchants or the commons, and the workmen or laborers ; and enables all human beings to attain happiness here as well as hereafter, by giving to each his due and not more than his due, dividing rights and duties, selfishness and unselfishness, work and play, equitably, and creating a balance of power between the main *classes* which make up every civilised community and are to the social organism even as the head, the hands, the trunk and the legs are to the individual living human body. This is the real meaning of the grand and utterly true old Vedic simile, now so misinterpreted and perverted from its true significance, by a combination of selfishness and ignorance, into the support of a system of blindly hereditary caste which only makes for arrogance and hypocrisy

---

duly circled round Him as all heavenly bodies must, to show respect. And she was so beautiful that Brahma Himself wanted to look at her all the time. Of course she was His own handiwork, and He had a right to be proud of her and admire her and say : " It is good." But then, He was expected, because of His anciency, to be grave, and not show curiosity like a little child ; it would be scandalous and give cause to the flippant and the wicked for vulgar laughter, if He got up and turned round and round also, to look at her. So the Mind sat still and created for itself faces with eyes on all four sides, and examined her carefully in all aspects and found the scheme flawless. Then He sent her forth on the mission for which she was specially created. And the two Titan brothers beheld her. It was a foregone conclusion. " I will have her." "No, I will have her." Each grabbed at the "Beautiful Grain-Heap." From words to blows is but a very small step. All their mutual brotherly love was gone in a moment. And soon their lives went too. The gods were happy

on the one hand and gullibility and ever-growing ingorance and then revolt on the other, and bitter internal dissensions and utter national weakness on all sides, in India.

It is for the establishment of Dharma in this largest and truest sense, whenever the balance of human society is jeopardised excessively by selfish, ruthless, evil and cruel human beings, that the great *avataras* appear, the Great Men of history in the fullest sense. In them the Oversoul puts forth its powers of good, to give right knowledge to humanity, inspire right desire and devotion to high ideals, and set example of noble action. Minor manifestations are called *avesha-s*, *amsha-s*, *kala-vatara-s*, *rshis*, *munis*, prophets, *nabi-s*, messiahs, sons of God, *rasul-s*, messengers of God, etc.; the greatest ones are called *avataras* proper, in Samskrt terminology.

The Puranas say that the central heart-and-brain of the solar system is the Sun, our *pratyaksha-devata*, " visible deity," the most radiant manifestation of the Spiritual Sun of the Gayatri-*mantra*.[10] His reverent invocation, for the *collective* mental illumination and inspiration, and therefore the physical and moral health, of the *community* (and not only of the *individual* worshipper) is the one indispensable and all-sufficient daily worship ordained for the regenerate, twice-born, Aryan person. He is the God in whose light and

---

again. They had their turn. " Every dog will have its day," and no more. Not the greatest cleverness will win immortality for the physical body of any single human being, or nation or race. Device always has been, always will be, countered by Nature Itself, *i.e.*, Universal Mind, with an anti-device which is already inherent in the device. The Spirit alone is Immortal.

[10]The Gayatri-mantra means: "May the effulgent glory of that God who is the Parent of all, inspire our minds rightly."

life we all literally live and move and have our being ; and from whose radiant *prana*-energy we obviously derive all our vitality and all our intelligence. In this Central Seed-and-Heart-and-Brain reside all the greatest wonders and forces;[11] It is the Oversoul of the whole solar system, and all the great avataras come from It in a peculiar sense. One scientific theory of the origin of life upon earth is that it came here from other heavenly bodies. The Puranas indicate that it came and continues to come, as need arises, from the Sun in a special degree, and that all the planets of the system exchange life-germs and souls from time to time even as the countries and the continents of this earth exchange inhabitants. This process was not confined to the distant past, but is going on now, for the Sun is not an absentee God, and his planets are not absentee angels, obviously.

---

[11]सर्वप्रवह्लिकानामाश्रयः । *Nirukta*. "The Sun is the centre of endless wonders, riddles, forces, mysteries."

सर्वदेवमनुष्याणां सरीसृपसवीरुधाम् ।
सर्वजीवनिकायानां सूर्य आत्मा दृग् ईश्वरः ॥

*Bhagavata*, V, xx, 46.

"The Sun is the en-livening soul, the inspiring intelligence, the sovereign lord, of vegetables, animals, humans, gods, etc., of all living things and beings, in short."

सर्वेषामवताराणां निधानं बीजमव्ययम् ।
यस्यांशांशेन सृज्यंते देवतिर्यङ्नरादयः ॥ *Bhagavata*.

"The inexhaustible seed-store of all avataras, out of a part of a part of Whom are made all gods and men and animals." सर्वदेवमयो हि सः, "He is made up of all the gods, *i.e.*, the more individualised high jivas as well as the less individualised nature-forces,"—*Bhagavata*. सूर्य आत्मा जगतस्तस्थुषश्च, "The Sun is the soul of the moving and the unmoving," —*Upanishat*.

And so the great avataras come from the Sun, [12] to this as well as to other planets. But minor manifestations arise otherwise. To take a familiar illustration : if a son or ward finds himself in difficulty in a distant land and informs the parent or guardian by wireless telegraphy, and the parent or guardian finds it necessary to travel down himself to save the situation, it may be technically said to be a case of an avatara proper. If he sends down a devoted friend or servant, it would be a *kala-vatara* or *amsha-vatara*. If he simply sends down instruction to a friend or agent on the spot, by means of telepathy, " inspires " him to do what is needed, it would be a case of *avesha*. And so on.

Also, the avataras and the anti-avataras usually come with their particular favorite groups, companies, *vyuhas*, of associates and friends (" boat-loads " in Theosophical literature). The old books mention the previous births and deeds of many of their main characters, and their changes of parts in the world-drama which they enliven. Thus Rama, the elder brother, devotedly served by Lakshmana, the younger, became Krishna, the younger brother, while the other, as Bala-rama, the elder, took his turn of ease. The other two brothers of Rama, namely Bharata and Shatrughna, became respectively Pradyumna and Aniruddha, the son and the grandson of Krishna.

Even in the case of Parashu-rama, though the current tradition briefly credits him with having " destroyed the Kshattriyas, root and branch, twenty-one times," single-handed, as it were, various Puranas, which describe his deeds more fully, say that his father Jamadagni and he gathered

---

[12] The *Bhavishya-Purana* has some explicit statements on the point and narrates specific instances.

great armies with which, at first the father, and after his death in battle at the hands of Kartavirya, the son, fought and broke the tyrannical militarism of his day in twenty-one great battles (as the legendary King Arthur of England, much later, defeated the enemies of his country in "twelve great battles"). The Kshattriyas of the Haihaya and the Tala-jangha ("long-legged") clans had obtained mastery over the land and lost all sense of right-and-duty, and begun to harass the people and to take away "the cow of Jamadagni," *i.e.*, their land and their means of living. (*Gauh*, now meaning only the cow, etymologically means whatever *goes*, *gachchhati iti gauh*, and in the earlier literature meant the ever-wandering orbs of heaven including the earth, the rushing rays of the sun, the five senses which are always going out to their objects, all kinds of cattle and not only the cow, and so forth). Well, Parashu-rama, a great avatara, seems to have done what is not usual in ancient Indian history; he gathered armies composed of *all the other three castes* and gave battle to the Kshattriyas. Usually, the work of fighting, and of providing to the world the dramatic scenes which break the monotony of life's dull routine, was left to be done by the Kshattriyas, as a mater of profession, while the rest of the people carried on the work of *their* respective professions. But in the time of Parashu-rama, necessity had to override the custom and everybody had to lend a hand.

The Kshattriyas whose duty it was to fight *for* the other three classes, had begun to fight *against* them. The policeman had become the thief. There was no outside true Kshattriya, sufficiently powerful, available to correct these. So there was no help but that the citizens at large should take up arms.

At first the allied armies were defeated, day after day.

Then, one night, a deputation went over to the Kshattriya camp and asked them: "We are many, you are few by comparison. How is it you manage to defeat us?" And the Kshattriyas, with the reckless dare-devil chivalry which still ran through their tyrannousness, replied: "You are a mob, each fighting for himself; we are an organised army, with a generalissimo, and the whole fights as one body under one head." Then the allies appointed Parashu-rama their generalissimo,[13] and steadily defeated the Kshattriyas. (The story is given in the Udyoga-parva of the *Maha-bharata*, but without the name of Parashu-rama.) Afterwards, when a genuine righteous-minded Kshattriya came, *viz.*, Rama, the aged Parashu-rama "handed over his bow," *i.e.*, his duty and his authority, to him, and the avataric afflatus passed from the elder to the younger Superman.

## Great Men of Thought, of Emotion, and of Action

Because there are three main functions of life and mind, therefore there are three main departments of human communal life and administration, three main features or aspects in every civilisation and culure, three main classes of work requiring to be fostered and promoted, three main sorts of disorder requiring to be cured, and three main kinds of Great Men that appear to cure them.

(*a*) When false teachers and false teachings which would elevate the things of the flesh above the things of the spirit begin to prevail; when erroneous notions of a gross kind,

---

[13]As also happened in the recent Great War in Europe, A.D. 1914-1918, when the French and the British, etc., had to appoint Marshal Foch as Generalissimo.

and false outlooks upon life, and ideals of mammonism and sensuousness, which would drag men away entirely from their birthright of the Eternal Spirit, threaten to undermine the foundations of civilisation and social organisation, by leading towards an excess of greed and grab and struggle and war and general lawlessness and anarchy: then the *teachers* appear to reillumine the Science of the Spirit and infuse the beauty of the ideal into the coarseness of the real. All the great seers, poets, philosophers and scientists of all lands and ages are high or low manifestations of these. Vyasa, Shankara, and the *shastra-pravartaka* Rshis, the fathers of learning, the discoverers and builders and "promulgators of new sciences" or revivers of old ones, are examples in Indian history. King Prthu,[14] *adi-raja,* the "first of kings," *raja-raja,* the "king of kings," an avatara of Vishnu, is a special combination of teacher and leader. Many of the fundamental arts of civilisation, as we know it to-day, were discovered and taught by him (so say the Puranas), or through appropriate teachers, in his glorious reign–the arts of agriculture with artificial irrigation, rearing of milch-cattle, music, house-building, town-laying, and many other arts of "milking the Earth-Cow" of her countlessly varied riches, as also various ill things, like the preparation of spirituous liquors, for every shine has its shadow. (*Bhagavata,* IV, xviii.)

मर्वे स्वमुख्यवत्सेन स्वे स्वे पात्रे पृथक् पयः ।
सर्वकामदुघां पृथ्वीं दुदुहुः पृथुभाविताम् ।।
चूर्णयन् स्वधनुष्कोटचा गिरिकूटानि राजराट् ।।
भूमंडलमिदं वैन्यः प्रायश्चक्रे समं विभुः ।।

[14]It is curious that the name sounds like "Pharaoh". Prthu was married to his sister Archi, say the Puranas. This is the solitary instance of such a marriage in the Human Dynasties mentioned in the Puranas;

अथास्मिन् भगवान् वैन्यः प्रजानां वृत्तिदः पिता ।
निवासान् कल्पयांचक्रे तत्र तत्र यथार्हतः ।।
प्राक् पृथोरिह नैवासीत् पुरग्रामादिकल्पना।
यथासुखं वसंतिस्म तत्र तत्राकुतोभयाः ।।

"The Lord Prthu, son of Vena, king of kings, caring for his people as a father for his children, crushed the hills, levelled the earth, built houses—for there were none before his day, and the people lived about as they pleased, wherever they could—and enabled the various groups of his people to milk from the Earth-Cow, under his supervision, whatever they wished, according to their respective tastes, through their group-leaders."

(*b*) When wrong emotions, the lower passions, false worships of over-sensuous gods, and the causes that increase lust, hate, greed, pride and the others of the brood of "the six inner enemies" spoken of in the Samskrt *shastras*, or "the seven deadly sins" of Christian theology, begin to grow and multiply, then the devotion-inspiring manifestations occur, who by their own love-compelling purity, nobility, humility and genuine self-effacement draw the hearts of human beings, and then diligently direct them, not towards themselves, not towards the forms of flesh and blood that they inhabit, but towards the Universal Fount

---

though it was the ordinary custom of the Egyptian Pharaohs to marry their sisters. There is some reason to think that, in the Puranas, the name of a person stands for a whole race or country. The Puranas mention many cases of "incestuous" marriage among the "gods"; but then the god-names are often, even obviously, names of abstract principles. They were lightly and transparently anthropomorphised by the sages for popular understanding, but unfortunately the metaphysical and allegorical meanings have been forgotten, and literalism is the order of the degenerate day.

of all Life. Mahavira Jina, Buddha, Christ, Ramanuja, Kabir, Sur, Tulasi, Chaitanya, Nanak and others, in various degrees, may be regarded as types of this class of manifestations; though Buddha and Jina, like Laotze and Confucius were great philosophical and intellectual teachers also.

(*c*) When wrong knowledge and wrong desire have not been cured in time, but have gained the upper hand—in accordance with the deeper laws that underlie the sequence of vicious as well as virtuous experiences that must be passed through by the human race and its sub-races—when the forces of evil selfishness and ruthless ambition, in the shape of cruelly selifish men, have obtained and held sway for their appointed term, gained by previous self-sacrifice and *tapasya*, then the history-making avataras proper appear, the adjusters of national Karma, the righters of widespread wrongs.[15]

It may be noted, in passing, that great men of action and great men of thought and science often, or even generally, appear together and help one another. Krishna and Vyasa make an outstanding illustration. Alexander and Aristotle, Cromwell and Milton, Akbar and Birbal, Shiva-ji and Ramdas, are others. The Elizabethan age in England, and the present age in Europe, also illustrate the same rule on a more voluminous and less individualised scale. Knowledge and action, theory and practice, obviously need each other. Every great movement has its philosopher as well as its active leader. And the sounder the philosophy which

[15]In Sufism we have the expressions *Nabi-ul-wilayat*, "the prophet of saintliness," the sage-saint, the *Atm-opadeshaka Rshis*, and *Nabi-ul-tashri*, the prophet of *shara*, of "institutions," the "institutors of laws," the *Smrti-kara Rshis*.

guides it the more helpful to humanity and the more lasting in results the movement. The *bhaktas*, devotees, and their Ideals, are more "self-sufficient," in a sense.

### Examples

Parashu-rama, Rama and Krishna are the outstanding examples of the history-makers, in ancient Indian History. The prophet Muhammad, founder of a religion and a law-giver as well as warrior and head of a state, is a good example in the history of other lands ; Guru Govinda Simha is another example, of a great man of action as well as spiritual teacher and poet of very high quality in modern Indian history.

The deeds of the ancient Indian avataras, mentioned above, are thrown into contrasting relief by the equally vast misdeeds of Kartavirya and the Haihayas, of Ravana and the Rakshasas, of Shishupala and Duryodhana and the Kauravas. All these names are, from the modern standpoint, prehistoric. Whether and which of the historic conquerors and Empire-founders and state-builders, *e.g.*, Meners, Minos, Chandragupta, Ashoka, Vikrama, Rameses, Solomon, Cyrus, Semiramis, Shi-Hwang-Ti, Hideyoshi, Iyeyasu, Alexander, Caesar, Attila, Changez, Tamer-lane, Akbar, Shivaji, Napoleon, Chaka of the Zulus, etc., should be regarded as manifestations on the right side or the wrong side—history cannot quite clearly make up its mind.[16] Even the purest lives, have touches of impurity ; even the worst have gleams of goodness; much more so these very mixed characters; because all are

[16]Historians too, like votaries, have their preferences and prejudices, their favorites and their pet aversions. Some, *f.i.*. would give the palm for supreme genius to Hannibal; others would bestow the laurel on Julius Caesar; some regard Napoleon as incomparable; others place Alexander

complexes of inseparable Spirit and Matter ; but Khalifa Ali, Rana Pratap, Cromwell, George Washington, Bolivar, Lincoln are generally acknowledged to be good as well as great names which stand for great and high ideals consistently fought for and upheld to the last ; and Ashoka is beginning to be given, by even western writers, a higher place, for goodness as well as greatness, than all other known monarchs of history, of East or West,[17] though he began his reign with the very cruel conquest of Kalinga, the sight of the horrors

---

above and beyond all others. Merivale, apparently with approval' (describing the *Breviarium* compiled by Augustus Caesar as a record of his own life-work), says:"The record extends over a period of fifty-eight years, and the great deeds it enumerates are certainly not to be equalled by the achievements of any other hero of ancient or modern history" (*History of Rome*, ch. liii). Gibbon, in his great work, can never mention Augustus Caesar without a depreciatory epithet. Mommsen, closing his account of Julius Caesar, says: "Thus he worked and created as never any mortal did before or after him; and as a worker and creator he still, after wellnigh two thousand years, lives in the memory of the nations" (*History of Rome*, Bk. V, ch.xi). H.G. Wells, in his *Outline of History*, characterises Alexander as a megalo-maniacal bounder and, occasionally, a brutal beast; and not without good reason, praises the Emperor Ashoka as the greatest and best ruler in all history. Hundreds of such, and greater, and better, and more evil, heroes, geniuses, conquerors, sovereigns, now all forgotten, have appeared in the long story of the Earth, in the midst of the hundreds of past races and nations and civilisations all equally forgotten. But the great types have been preserved in the Permanent History of the World, the Purana, and they recur again and again on larger or smaller scales. (See the *Bhagavata*, XII,iii, and *The Science of the Emotions*, pp. 459-460, foot-note.)

[17]H. G. Wells, *Outline of History;* and A.R. Cowan, *A Guide to World-History*, p. 172 (pub. 1923): "Ashoka's . . . is, in its way, the most imposing figure that ever adorned a human dynasty. If a man's fame, says Koppen, can be measured by the number of hearts who revere his

of which were, indeed, the cause of his heart-conversion. Only the predominant quality gives the name. And this, by the way, is a most important metaphysical axiom, which, taken together with its brother axiom, that every question has two sides and the true answer always lies in the mean between the two extremes, solves many an otherwise insoluble puzzle. Thus the threefold classification of Great Men is only by predominance ; none has been exclusively and wholly either a teacher, or a devotion-inspirer, or a history-maker. Every new re-lig-ion, every re-bind-ing together of human hearts, by Manu, Buddha, Moses, Christ, Muhammad, or Shankara, Ramanuja, Chaitanya, Guru Govinda Simha, whether by philosophical teaching or by devotion-inspiring, has been followed, as said before, by a new civilisation, a new culture, and new states, larger or smaller in space and time ; though, of course, the religions, and the corresponding cultures, have, in all cases, managed, in the course of time, to drift away very far from the ideals of the founders and reformers, in consequence of the drag of the lower half of human nature upon the higher, and the same old degenerative superstitions and vices have re-appeared in every one, under new forms.

But while most of these Great Men have discharged one function predominantly, Krishna seems to have combined in himself all the three functions in an extraordinary degree. His activities and perfections were so many-sided that he is claimed by a very large section of the Hindu people to have been a *purna-avatara*, " a *complete* manifestation," of the *whole* of the Supereme or rather Universal Life, as no other was, not even Rama himself.

---

memory and the lips who have mentioned, and still mention, him with honor, Ashoka is more famous than Charlemagne or Caesar."

कृष्णस्तु भगवान् स्वयम्। In his teaching too, Krishna duly followed the path laid down by Manu, and was all-sided and balanced : giving its proper place to every duty, every desire, every ideal ; not making any extremist demand, as some religion-founders had to do because of special circumstances.

Yet this is but the natural (and though excusable yet mischievous) exaggeration of loving and devoted hearts which, deceived into subtle pride by the very sweetness of this form of Maya, cannot rest content till they have magnified and glorified their own particular favorite deity or hero or ideal beyond all others, thereby implicitly belittling all the others.[18] That the *whole* of the Infinite Universal Spirit cannot be exhaustively focussed into any one finite part, however great, is mathematically obvious. And in this particular case, the *Bhagavata* itself says that Bala-rama and Krishna were " two threads of hair," one white and one dark, two strands from the locks, two rays from the coronal aureole, of the head of *Aditya-Narayana*, the Sun, the very

[18]So, good Christians insist that Jesus is the only begotten Son of God; and orthodox Musalmans are positive that their prophet Muhammad is higher than all the angels and next only after God. The element of truth in the statements, or rather the feelings, of all three is one and the same; *viz.*, that Krishna-Vasudeva, and Christos, and Haqiqat-i-Muhammadi, all three mystically mean the Buddhi-Mahat (of Sankhya), the primal manifestation, as Universal Mind, of the Supreme Self. This is expressly stated in the *Bhagavata*, and in the mystic and Sufi books respectively. From another stand-point, it may be said, in colloquial language, that no one is good for nothing, nor is anyone good for everything, and the claims made for Krishna amount only to this that he was good for more and finer and stronger things than any of his known contemporaries (or, some may even add, precessors and successors in history).

visibly obvious Head of our solar system. सितकृष्णकेशौ is the expression used.[19] Members of the vast Spiritual Hierarchy are spoken of as "hairs," "beads of the neck-lace," etc., of the Sun referred to under one or another of the forms of the Divine Trinity, the Tri-murti.

Rama and Krishna divide the heart of the Hindu people between them. Even Vyasa, the great contemporary and historian of Krishna and his time, who has composed that marvellous Epic of Devotion, the *Bhagavata*, in praise and adoration of Krishna pre-eminently —even Vyasa reserves a place, in his heart, of very tender reverence for Rama the Perfect, the Noble, the *Maryada-Purusha*, the "Standard Man" ***par excellence.*** In every one of the many Puranas which tradition ascribes to Vyasa, the story of Rama is included as an episode, at greater or lesser length ; and in the *Bhagavata* itself he sings hymns to Rama whose wealth of feeling is not surpassed by those of his *stotras* to Krishna.

---

[19] Also the *Mahabharata*, Shanti-parva, ch, 206,

भूमेर्दुःखोपनाशार्थं ब्रह्मशक्रादिभिः स्तुतः ।
आत्मनोऽङ्गान्महातेजा उद्धवर्हं जनार्दनः ।
सितकृष्णौ महाराज केशौ हरिरुदारधीः ॥

And *Bhagavata*, X, ii, aud IV, ii,

अथाहमंशभागेन देवक्याः पुत्रनां शुभे ।
प्राप्स्यामि त्वं यशोदायां नन्दपन्न्या भविप्यसि ॥
भगवानपि विश्वात्मा भक्तानाम्भयंकरः ।
आविवेशांशभागेन मन आनकदुंदुभेः॥
ताविमौ वै भगवतो हरेरंशाविहागतौ ।
भारव्ययाय च भुवः कृप्णौ यदुकुलोद्वहौ ॥ etc.

त्यक्त्वा सुदुस्त्यजसुरेप्सितराज्यलक्ष्मीं
धर्मिष्ठ आर्यवचनाद् यदगादरण्यं ।
भृत्यार्तिहं प्रणतपाल भवाब्धिपोतं
वंदे महापुरुष ते चरणारविंदम् ॥

"I salute thy feet, O greatest of men !, most perfect in duty !, most tender, heroic and ever-resistless defender of thy devotees and dependents from all ills ! In all reverent humility I salute thy feet that lightly turned away, at the wish of the father, from the glories of a kingship which the gods themselves might envy, towards the depths of the wild forests. I salute the feet that guide the tired and the weary safely across the wilderness of life, as the ships carry merchants across the ocean of waters."

### The All-Sidedness of Krishna

But the devotion that Krishna inspires is different. The devotion inspired by Rama is as pure, simple, noble, straightforward, spiritual, transparent, deep, even-flowing, homely, artless, strong, as his own nature, his life, his love for Sita, for his parents, his brothers, his sons, his people, friends, servants, even his enemies. The devotion aroused by Krishna is intense, physical as well as superphysical and spiritual, complex, many-sided, maddening, transporting now with joy and now with sorrow, shaking the whole soul to pieces and yet always joining up the pieces again with Love and Life and Light Eternal—like his own life, his loves, his deeds, his age and his surroundings.

As western anothropologists have divided Man's lifetime into the Stone age, the Bronze age, the Iron age, etc., in terms of the external implements used by him ; as socio-political historians of post-Roman national life in Europe have divided the Christian Centuries into the Dark Age, the Mediaeval Age, the Renaissance Period, and the Modern Age, so Puranic historians have divided the long Story of Man into the Satya, the Treta, the Dvapara and the Kali eras,[20] in terms of man's psychological and ethical characteristics. They add the clear explanation that while the Yugas succeed one another in and for any given country and people, they are coexistent if different countries and peoples are taken into account simultaneously. This, in the modern phrase of the evolutionary sociologist, means that all the stages of man's social development are to be found to-day in different parts of the earth. Rama came to wind up the Treta age,[21] wherein love and co-operation and unselfishness are almost as three parts, and struggle and selfishness as one, and gave a last great illustration of the patriarchal administration of the affairs of men at its best. The preceding or Satya age might be regarded as one of primitive joint-family-like communism, wherein unselfish love and trust and mutual help are almost unopposed, and sin and selfishness are next to nil. Krishna came at the junction between Dvapara and

---

[20]*Satya* means "truth"; the age is also known as *Krta*, "action," *i.e.*, the age in which the people *did* unquestioningly what their benevolent elders told them. *Treta* means "three," the third age, counting backwards from the present; also the age in which the feelings and forces of good are as three parts, and those of evil as one; also the age in which people were specially "protected," *trayate*, by their elders. *Dva-para* means "two-sided," hence doubt also. *Kali* means "discord," "struggle".

[21]Of the Aryan Race; it has to be remembered that different Ages prevail for different Races in different countries at the same time. Thus Ravana was the contemporary and enemy of Rama and his Rakshasa Race can scarcely be said to have been in the Satya Yuga then. Probably it was in its Dva-para, or maybe, the Kali.

Kali, when the latter, the age of predominant individualism and competition and "struggle", was beginning, and the former, that of almost equal "duality," equal sin and virtue, equal competition and co-operation, was coming to[22] an end. The Maha-bharata war, which Krishna conducted, is typical of this age. The whole atmosphere of Krishna is far more stormy, passionate, complex, than that of Rama. He is the typical perfect individual appropriate to this age of intense, concentrated, all-round activity—great in knowledge, great in emotion, great in action, all together. The available Scriptures and the literatures of mankind do not seem to record any life fuller and more intense than his.

## KRISHNA AS MAN OF ACTION AND HISTORY-MAKER AND RIGHTER OF WRONGS

The *Bhagavata Purana* says that he was born five thousand years ago, in round figures, at the close of the Dvapara and the beginning of the Kali age, and "lived for one hundred and twenty-five years on earth" (XI, vi, 25),[23]

यदुवंशेऽवतीर्णस्य भवतः पुरुषोत्तम ।
शरच्छतं व्यतीयाय पंचविंशाधिकं प्रभो ॥

[22]In some Puranas, epochs are distinguished as those of *Apas-Siddhi*, "Water-resource," *Vrksha-Siddhi*, "Tree-resource," and *Hasta-Siddhi*, "Hand-accomplishment," *i.e.*, the Ages, respectively, in which men got their necessaries (1) from the water, fish, cresses, seeds of aquatic flowers, etc., for food, turtle-shells, etc., for implements, and so on; (2) from the vegetable kingdom, roots and fruits for food, leaves and bark and fibres for clothing, wood and leaves, grass and straw, for fuel and huts and thatching and bedding, etc., and (3)from skill of hand, with "opposable thumbs." in manufacture.

[23]But the *Maha-bharata*, Adi-parva, ch. 134, (Kumbakonam Edn.), says that Yudhishthira lived for one hundred and eight years, that Bhima

In every week of this period, if not on every day of it, he fought and battled and warred against and slew evil-doers. As a few-weeks-old baby he bit to death the ogress Putana, sent to murder him with poison-painted breasts by his maternal uncle Kamsa who had been forewarned by the sensation-loving, drama-making Rshi, Narada, that he was destined to be slain by his sister's son. On the very last day of his stay on earth, he slew with his own hands his kinsmen who, before his eyes, slew his favorite pupil Satyaki and his favorite son Pradyumna in that awful drink-maddened mutual slaughter of the Yadavas on the seacoast of Prabhasa, at the close of the day. When he came, the people of the earth were groaning under the intolerable burdens of militarism and the abuse of power by those whose duty it was to protect and not oppress the weak. The Puranas and the *Gita* poetically describe the situation thus :

एवं वीर्यमदोत्सिक्तैर्भूरियं तैर् महासुरैः ।
पीड़िता भृशसंतप्ता जगाम प्रपितामहम् ।।
त्रिविधं नरकस्येदं द्वारं नाशनमात्मनः ।
कामः क्रोधस्तथा लोभस्तस्मादेतत्त्रयं त्यजेत् ।।

---

was a year younger, Arjuna two years, and the twins Nakula and Sahadeva three years; and that Krishna was three months older than Arjuna, and Bala-rama three months older than (his step-brother) Krishna. And it was on hearing of Krishna's departure from the earth, that the five brothers put their grandson Parikshit on the throne, and went away and cast off their bodies in the "desert beyond the Himalayas, to the north, and in sight of the Meru Mountain". (*Ibid.*, Maha-prasthanika-parva, ch. 2.) By this calculation Krishna's stay on this earth would come to about one hundred and five or six rather than one hundred and twenty-five years.

" Oppressed beyond endurance by those Titans born as rulers of men, mad with the lust of power, the Earth went and cried her agony before the Lord of the Universe ; for the rule of the Titan-souls, that had been born into the human forms of the kings of the time, was leading the populations of the earth towards the hell of which lust, hate, and greed form the yawning triple gateway."

The Kshattriya rulers were as ruthless as the Asuras and Rakshasas—by which terms men of the Atlantean and Mongolian races seem to be meant—who had established themselves in strongholds here and there in the country and were harassing the people. Many of these latter he slew with his own hands, others he got slain by Bhima and Arjuna. As he says in the *Maha-bharata* :

रावणेन समप्राणा मया भीमेन घातिताः ।

" I have had these, who were of equal vitality with Ravana himself, slain by Bhima."

After slaying Kamsa, king of Mathura, Krishna restored to the throne the deposed and aged Ugra-sena, father of Kamsa, and tried to carry on the kingdom at Mathura itself. But he found the work of peaceful administration and promotion of the people's welfare impossible to do. The kings and chiefs of the neighboring countries were too turbulent, too despotic and autocratic. Especially Jara-sandha,[24]

---

[24]Jara-sandha is an early example of the ambitious king, not common in Indian Legend, who, mad with lust for exclusive power, tries to eradicate all oligarchical and republican spirit in his domains, and convert his state into a pure autocracy, an absolute monarchy. He collected, in his prisons, *sixteen thousand* chiefs and nobles, all of whom he intended to "sacrifice" and slaughter outright in one great holocaust. They were

father-in-law of Kamsa, and ruler of the very powerful kingdom of Magadha, waged unquenchable vendetta against him. He attacked Mathura seventeen times and was driven away defeated each time. The eighteenth time he secured for ally a powerful Yavana (Ionian?) Chief with immense hordes of fighting followers. Krishna managed to get the Yavana Chief slain by Muchukunda (who has a story of his own) ; but decided on a great migration. He went over with all his people, to the shores of the western sea at Dwaraka, a thousand miles away, across mountains and great stretches of desert sand. There he created a greater city, on the site of an old one. In it he established a sort of republic, a *sangha-rajya*, or an oligarchy, a *gana-rajya*, or a compound of the two, an oligarchical republic, (there are not yet enough materials available to ascertain exactly which, but most probably the last), known as the Andhaka-Vrshnayah, after the names of the two most important of the clans, which, as a whole, were called the Yadavas, and included the Kukuras, the Bhojas, the Satwatas, etc., also. Apparently he hoped that they would behave better, as such an oligarchical republic, than the autocratic despots. If so, his hope was not fulfilled. The strain of turbulence, the traditions, the temper, and the training of violence, were not to be eardicated so easily, by a change in the mere form of government. The spirit, the wrong spirit, of the fight-ravenous if chivalrous, the blood-thirsty if generous, Kshattriyas remained. There were also the many relations of all kinds, marital, social, commercial, etc., between the new

---

ultimately rescued by Krishna, Arjuna, and Bhima, after slaying Jarasandha. No subsequent Roman emperor or Persian "king of kings" or French king could outmatch him, apparently!

semi-republic and the old monarchical states on all sides. The evil called for a more radical remedy.[25]

Krishna therefore utilised the bitter personal quarrels between the two groups of cousins, the Pandavas and the Kauravas, with both of whom he and his kinsmen had close matrimonial alliances, for the bringing about of a war on an immense scale in which the militarists would destroy each other, like Sunda and Upa-sunda.

And he gathered together, by consummate statesmanship, all the inextricably intermingled forces of evil and of good of his day, at one time and place, on the plains of Kuru-kshetra, and hurled them against each other with such skill that though at the beginning of the battle the evil forces outweighed the good ones by eleven *akshauhinis* to seven, *i.e.*, about 2½ millions to 1½, at the end of it, the proportion was three survivors on the side of might to seven on the side of right.[26] Finally, knowing that the Kuru-kshetra had not completed all his work, Krishna finished it at Prabhasa-kshetra, on the shores of the sea of Dwaraka, when his immediate kith and kin slaughtered each other to the number of half a million, as said in the *Maha-bharata*, drunk with alcohol and even more drunk with the arrogance of militarism. In this way he broke the last great and dangerous

---

[25]Compare the conditions of Europe and America in the years before, during, and after the Great War of A.D. 1914-1918. France and the U.S.A. were great republics, and, when the war began, there were two republics included also among the twenty-three states which made up the German Empire.

[26]An *akshauhini* is a force consisting of 21,870 chariots, 21,870 elephants 65,610 horsemen, 109,350 foot-soldiers; and Duryodhana had eleven such and Yudhishthira seven.

military power of his day and gave to the peaceful agriculturist and tradesman a chance.[27] His voyages for the breaking of militarists across the seas, in other continents and islands, are also recorded in other Puranas.[28]

After the figures of the greater war, which closed with the armistice of November, 1918, and the peace-treaties of 1919, wherein at least eight millions (and, by some calculations, so many as thirteen) were slaughtered outright and at least as many mutilated and maimed for life, these figures of those previous wars will not be doubted as fanciful. By them, the Ancient Law, Sanatana Dharma, became able to hold up its head for another 2,500 years.

Then it degenerated again, and diseased with age. Then the Buddha came to reform it with special insistence on rationality, co-operation, righteousness, non-violence,

---

[27]ये कोपिताः सुबहु पांडुसुताः सपत्न –
दुर्द्यूतहेलनकचग्रहणादिभिस्तान्।
कृत्वा निमित्तमितरेतरतः समेतान्
हत्वा नृपान्निरहरत् क्षितिभारमीशः ॥
भूभारराजपृतना यदुभिर्निरस्य
गुप्तैः स्वबाहुभिरचिंतयदप्रमेयः ।
मन्येऽवनेर्ननु गतोऽप्यगतं हि भारो
यद्यादवं कुलमहो ह्यविषह्यमास्ते ॥
नैवान्यतः परिभवोऽस्य भवेत्कथंचिन्
मत्संश्रयस्य विभवोन्नहनस्य नित्यम् ।
अंतः कलिं यदुकुलस्य विधाय वेणु–
स्तम्बस्य वह्निमिव शांतिमुपैमि धाम ॥

*Bhagavata*, XI, i, 2-3-4.

[28]*Hari-vamsha. Garga-Samhita, Brahma-vaivarta.*

and renunciation, and gave it another lease of life for a thousand years in India. "I seek and find refuge in the Buddha, the Wise, *i.e.*, in the Eternal Spiritual Wisdom. I find refuge in the Dharma, in the Code of Life, the Law (materio-spiritual) which arises from that Wisdom. I find refuge in the Sangha, the Organised Society (human and hierarchical, as included in the universal), which arises from that Law."[29]

When it grew corrupt again, Shankara and Ramanuja and others took up the work of reform and revival. Others have arisen in more recent times. The work of world-mending is un-ending. For the forces of re-form and de-form are both simultaneously and perpetually at work. Now the one prevails and now the other.

Such then was Krishna's principal work as man of action and maker of history. His many youthful deeds of daring, his battles with and destruction of dangerous beasts and birds and reptiles, vicious horses, mad bulls, ferocious vultures, pythons and snakes, monstrous birds and reptiles of the diornis and the dragon or kraken (saurian) type, (a few of which seem to have been still living[30] in caves five thousand years ago, as remnants from the earlier ages), and also robbers, in the hills and the caves, the forests and the streams, neighboring his adoptive father Nanda's ranch ; his pro-

---

[29] बुद्धं शरणं गच्छामि, धर्मं शरणं गच्छामि, संघं शरणं गच्छामि ।

[30] Some four-tusked mammoths were brought by the King Bhaga-datta of Prag-jyotisha (Assam) to the Great War. चतुर्दन्ता इभास्तस्य । *Mahabharata*, and

ऐरावतकुलेभांश्च चतुर्दतांस्तरस्विनः। पांडुरांश्च चतुःषष्टि प्रेषयामास केशवः॥
*Bhagavata*, *X,lx.*

tection of his fellow-cowkeeper-boys and their flocks and herds from violent thunderstorms which lasted whole weeks, with the help of a great cave he had discovered in the Govardhana hills—all these have formed the theme of much devotional and idealised, fancifully exaggerated and mysticalised, poetry that serves " to point a moral and adorn a tale." We must content ourselves here with only a passing mention of it. And yet, for purposes of illustration, something more may be said. The serpent Kaliya has been frequenting the banks and "poisoning" the waters of the Yamuna. Krishna, a mere boy at the time, leaps into the river one day, when Kaliya is swimming, to fight the reptile out. The great snake rushes at him with uplifted head. Krishna drags the head down under water, the snake is almost drowned, and wriggles out, and runs away for good. But this simple story is not enough. Some Puranas make out that Kaliya had five heads on which Krishna danced triumphantly; they perhaps mean that the soul may and ought to reign over the five senses. The *Bhagavata* goes further and describes in beautiful poetic language, how " The Eternal Boy, first Master of all Arts, danced on the hundred heads and one of that great snake, stamping with all-subduing might now on this and now on that grim head, as it rose hissing, rebellious and menacing—till they were all battered, humbled, and reduced to due submission, and prayed to be allowed to go in peace."

यद्यच्छिरो न नमतेऽङ्ग शतैकशीर्ष्णं-
स्तत्तन्ममर्द खरदंडधरोंघ्रिपातैः ।
तन्मूर्धरत्ननिकरस्पर्शातिताम्र-
पादाम्बुजोऽखिलकलादिगुरुर्ननर्त्त ॥

It is probably referring to the hundred and one principal

*nadis* or nerves of the human nervous system mentioned in the Upanishats, every one of which is supposed to come under the definite and perfect control of the practised and perfected *yogi*, advanced type of future humanity. And it probably does so for weaving into the story, mystical, philosophical, and scientific hints and suggestions, for the purposes of educative stimulation of curiosity and enquiry. Some other scholars are inclined to interpret the Kaliya episode as an allegory of the putting down of serpent-worship which also, they say, was over-prevalent then. But if so, then we have to add that the law of history, *viz.*, that the conquerors are often conquered by the conquered, in other ways, is illustrated in this instance also. Bala-rama came to be regarded as an incarnation of the Eternal Snake, Ananta, the " Endless " spiral Force.[31]

## Krishna as Man of Emotion and Devotion-Inspirer

As man of desire, of feeling, of arts, Krishna's life was equally full.

The *shastras* say that the *summum bonum* of human life is dual ; first *Abhyudaya,* then *Nis-shreyas ;* first the joys of the embodied life (inseparable from some degree of " sin "), and then the bliss of " salvation," the realisation of the oneness of the individual with the Universal Spirit, the satisfaction of the hunger and thirst of the soul for God, of the

[31] Archaeologists say that the Naga cult seems to have flourished at Mathura (first, second, and third centuries A.D.) and the later images of Bala-rama are identical with and derived from these Naga types; figures of Nagas and Yakshas both in the round and as reliefs are commonly found.

longing of the river for the sea, of the moth for the star, of the part for the whole, of the finite for the Infinite—satisfaction by the assurance that I am (that every I is) the eternal, infinite, universal I. The first is subdivided into Dharma, Artha, Kama; that is to say, *kama*, or the joys of sense-life must be refined by *artha* or the riches of art, which riches must be gathered and spent and administered in accordance with, and can be duly guarded only by, *dharma* or law and order.

The same *shastras* mention the conditions of the fulfilment of each end thus :

अर्थस्य मूलं निकृतिः क्षमा च कामस्य रूपं च वयो वपुश्च ।
धर्मस्य यागादि दया दमश्च मोक्षस्य सर्वोपरमः क्रियाभ्यः ॥

" The prime requisites for the due fulfilment of the end of *kama* or 'pleasure' are strength, beauty and youth ; of *artha* or 'wealth,' they are non-arrogant patience and artful ways ; of *dharma* or 'duty' or order in liberty, they are sacrifice, self-control, compassion for the weak ; of *moksha* or 'salvation,' the one condition is retirement from the activities of the world."

But one requisite, more essential than all others, without which all others remain unfulfilled, ineffective, has been, so far, in the history of mankind, possible only in the very rare cases of Krishna-s, born once in a long age (and then there have been other hindrances !). It is the requisite of mature and conscious wisdom, born of the remembered experience of previous lives. "Many have been our previous births," says Krishna to Arjuna, "I remember them all ; you do not." Beautiful and strong and youthful body, wealth unbounded, pious works—none of these yield up their full flavour to the *jiva*, unless they are guided by wisdom. Especially are the delicate sentiments, the vehement emotions, the deep heart-mysteries, of love, liable to go astray in youthful bodies, uncontrolled by knowledge, like the car of Phoebus in the hands of Phaethon. But the irony of fate ordains that experienced wisdom, which alone can make enjoyment perfect, shall begin to grow only when the body begins to decay, and that the body should be capable of enjoyment only when the mind is not. Let us hope that in the distant, if not the near, future, the combination of beautiful body and wise mind will be possible; the misfits, the mistakes, the misunderstandings, the mismatings of today will be avoided; and the race of man become a race of Krishna-s and Rukmini-s.

Krishna's extraordinary beauty of face and figure and unique color and complexion have been the theme of the singers of a hundred and fifty generations after him. That simple village-maidens or even conscious city-ladies should lose their hearts to him, that he should inspire compeers of his own sex with enthusiastic admiration and devoted affection—are not difficult to understand. But when Bhishma, belonging to the generation of Krishna's grandfather, Bhishma, much over a hundred years of age at that time, stretched on his death-bed of arrows, waiting for the right moment to cast off his body by *yoga*—when he, seeing Krishna standing before him, can think of nothing else for his first thought than Krishna's physical beauty, then we may well believe that it must have been something overpowering. In his dying hymn to Krishna, as avatara of Narayana, Bhishma sings first of his physical beauty : "The heart's desire of the three worlds, waking, dreaming and sleeping, (for is not the Self the Best Beloved of every self perforce ?), lovingly gazed on with tireless eyes by all beholders, the peculiar complexion, the splendid dress, the curling locks playing about the oval lotus-face, the loving glance, the thrilling voice, and the graces of smile and laugh and speech and gesture and every movement that drove the youths and maidens mad almost."

त्रिभुवनकमनं तमालवर्णं रविकरगौरवरांबरं दधाने ।
वपुरलककुलावृताननाब्जं विजयसखे रतिरस्तु मेऽनवद्या ॥
ललितगतिविलासवल्गुहास-
प्रणयनिरीक्षणकल्पितोरुमानाः ।
कृतमनुकृतवत्य उन्मदांधाः
प्रकृतिमगन् किल यस्य गोपवध्वः ॥

The body is obviously the soul made visible. In the case of Krishna, this truth is verified amply by his marvellous aesthetic taste and mastery of the "sixty-four" fine and other arts. He began as a flute-player, fascinating the village maids and youths and the cattle and the animals of the jungle. He ended with giving lessons to specialist and expert Narada in the art of playing the *vina*. It may be noted, in passing, that Krishna's own "schooling" with the Acharya Sandipani, originally belonging to Benares, but settled at Ujjain, is an object-lesson in the science of education. He went there with his brother Bala-rama, many hundreds of miles distant from his paternal home in Mathura, after he had come away from Vrndavana, and had slain his parent's and his own and the people's enemy, King Kamsa, and become famous ; and he lived and studied with his teacher just like the other nameless students, in respect of the *hardy life* ; gathering fuel from the woods for his teacher's household fires ; getting " lost " with companions, and wandering about in the jungle for whole nights, in thunderstorms, inspiring those companions, as usual, with lifelong love, unlike them only in his powers of body and mind, and astonishing his teacher with the quality of his memory, wonderful like all things else of his, retaining the most difficult learning after but one hearing. To build up hardy body and determined mind, to develop courage to overmaster danger, to perfect oneself in the " discipline " fit for a worthy disciple, the training which cultivates the intellect and the emotions, *i.e.* builds up a fine character, to acquire the power and the habit of doing all one's work oneself without dependence on dependents, to lay the foundations of lifelong friendships, to learn about and duly exercise both *rights* and *duties*, to gain admission into all the departments of science and art, to understand what the ends of life are and how to achieve them—that this is the purpose of Education is illustrated by Krishna's " schooling."

अथो गुरुकुले वासमिच्छन्तावुपजग्मतुः ।
काश्यं सान्दीपनिं नाम ह्यवन्तिपुरवासिनम् ॥
तयोर्द्विजवरस्तुष्टः शुद्धभावानुवृत्तिभिः ।
प्रोवाच वेदानखिलान् सांगोपनिषदो गुरुः ॥

सरहस्यं धनुर्वेदं धर्मान्नयायपथांस्तथा ।
तथा चान्वीक्षिकीं विद्यां राजनीतिं च षड्विधाम् ॥
सर्वं नरवरश्रेष्ठौ सर्वविद्याप्रवर्त्तकौ ।
सकृन्निगदमात्रेण तौ संजगृहतुर्नृप ॥
अहोरात्रैश्चतुःषष्टया संयत्तौ तावतीः कलाः ।

*Bhagavata*, X, xlv.

"The Acharya Sandipani, pleased with their pure-minded dutifulness, expounded to the two glorious brothers, all the Vedas, together with their subsidiary sciences, and their quintessential secret, the philosophy of the Upanishats, also the sciences and the arts of war, of law, of logical reasoning, of politics and civics with their six departments. And the two wondrous mock-pupils, in reality the Ancient Creaters and Masters of all Sciences and Arts, seized hold of all these at one hearing, and mastered the sixty-four fine arts in as many days." The *Mahabharata* describes their "complete course of education" somewhat differently, thus: "In sixty-four days and nights they learnt all the Vedas, with all their, *Angas*. subsidiaries, and the art of writing, and mathematics and music, and medicine. In twelve days they mastered the science and the art of the Elephant and the Horse. In fifty days and nights they mastered the Scripture of the Bow, the Science and the Art of War, in all its ten departments" (*Sabha*, ch. 54).

Krishna reclaimed land from the ocean by a feat of engineering not detailed in the available books, unfortunately, but described poetically as consisting in a simple command to the ocean to recede; built his great city of Dwaraka near by, on the site of an ancient vanished capital-town; filled the city with towered and spired buildings, and constructed a hall of audience whose walls and pillars were inlaid with scores of different kinds of gems and jewels duly listed in the *Hari-vamsha*. This hall was named Sudharma and outrivalled even Yudhisthira's marvellous palace at Indraprastha, built by the Asura (probably Atlantean-Mongolian) architect,

Maya, also at Krishna's instance.[32] The Puranic descriptions of these vanished ancient buildings "designed by Titans and finished by jewellers" seem to have spurred Shah-jahan to emulation in the Taj Mahal.

His skill in the breeding and training of horses was such that the names of his four favorites have come down to us: Shaibya, Sugriva, Megha-pushpa and Balahaka. It seems that with the help of these he used to cover the distance between Indra-prastha (Delhi) and Dwaraka in a week, a *saptaha.* Kathiawari horses are even now famous for their going powers; and the *Brahma Purana* mentions by name a famous mare also of Krishna's time, belonging to Prasena, a relative of his.

वड़वा हृदया नाम शतयोजनगामिनी ।

"The mare, Hrdaya, which could go one hundred *yojanas* (equal to about 800 miles) continuously." Those who know of the long-distance riding feats, in the "bush," of Australian riders and their horses, will not feel sceptical.[33]

His favorite aeroplane was known as the Garuda,[34] with which he seems to have kept in constant touch by

[32] Many fine remains of the "Mayas" have been and are being discovered in Mexico, Honduras, etc., indicating a high civilisation combined with serpent-worship. The *Maha-bharata* says that Arjuna made a journey to "Naga (serpent)-loka," and married a Naga princess, Ulupi by name; and the architect and super-craftsman whose life he saved once was a special friend of his.

[33] Not many years ago the newspapers recorded a match in which a number of horses, under riders of course, managed to cover one thousand miles in ten days, in Australia, the minimum and maximum for single days being seventy and one hundred and thirty miles, respectively.

[34] Mr. K. V. Vaze, in his work on *The Philosophy of Ancient Indian Engineering* (published as a series of articles in the *Vedic Magazine*, of Gurukula Kangri), gives the Samskrit names of different kinds of air-vehicles.

means of some wireless telegraphy—as the big air-ship of one of his most implacable enemies, Shalva (whom he ultimately destroyed together with the air-ship), was known as the Saubha.

He introduced new flowers like the *parijata* into the country, undertaking even a sharp little war for the purpose, which the books hyperbolically speak of as a war with Indra,[35] to bring away the plant from "heaven" (some other country of the earth, especially fine in those days, seems to be meant), at the instigation of his very favorite and very forward wife Satyabhama. His care and taste in dress are shown by the fact that he generally wore yellow silk, as his elder brother, Bala-rama, wore blue. In those days they knew and took care to select the color that suited their complexions,[36] for

[35]Could the Indra. in this case, be anyone like the Inca of Peru, with his splendid gardens, wherein living trees alternated with artificial ones of gold ?

[36]Bala-rama was very white which is well understood; but Krishna seems to have had some extra-ordinary color which the old books dwell on frequently and try to present to the mental vision of the reader or hearer by means of many similes, now the *atasi*-linseed flower, now the new rain-cloud, now the emerald, now the sapphire. A great many Indian babies are born to-day with a patch of *greenish-bluish* tint on the lower portion of the back, extending over the nates, which is very pretty if the general color of the baby is fair white or yellowish-golden. If that tint could be spread all over the body, it would make a Krishna. There is an anthropological theory about this tint-patch on babies, that it means a mixture of Mongol blood in the past; but whether well- or ill-founded is not yet settled. Herr Baelz has propounded the theroy. It is said that every Chinese, every Korean, Japanese, and Malay is born with a dark blue patch of irregular shape in the lower sacral region: and that these patches generally disappear in the first year of life, but sometimes they last for several years. It is worth enquiring whether any European babies also have such patches, as a matter of anthropology; and *why* they occur, and disappear, as a matter of physiological chemistry.

the cult of physical masculine beauty—to say nothing of feminine, which was a matter of course—was fairly widespread in that day. Krishna's son Pradyumna and grandson Aniruddha (reincarnations of Bharata and Shatrughna) and cousin Nakula were other famously handsome men of the time, next only after Krishna; and the *Mahabharata* describes many other men of grand physique.

He married eight wives, carefully selected, and every one of them won by a great feat of strength or courage (and had many "affairs of the heart" besides). He built a magnificent palace for each of these eight queens.[37] The *Mahabharata*, Sabha-parva, ch. 57, gives a gorgeous description, with the name, of each. While in sheer size of thews and sinews and strength of muscle, four men were noted beyond the common in his day, yet still such was the miracle of Krishna's vital vigor that even in this respect he was regarded as simply above and beyond comparison.

The *Maha-bharata* says :

सांप्रतं मानुपे लोके सदैत्यनरराक्षमे ।
चत्वारस्तु नरव्याघ्रा बले शक्रोपमा भुवि ॥

---

[37]The Puranas say they were "goddesses" incarnated on earth, by order of Brahma, "to rejoice Krishna's heart and vivify him" for his immense labors, Rukmini, his first and principal wife. being. of course, a piece of Lakshmi herself.

ग्रानंदनाय कृष्णस्य देव्यस्ना भुवमागताः ।

A happy love is aliment for soul and body both; as one-sided lust is poison. A letter from the then faithful Napoleon to his unhappily then faithless wife Josephine, says: "The charm of the incomparable Ludwig is perpetually re-kindling the flames of my heart and henses Ludwig, *Napoleon*, p. 74).

उत्तमप्राणिनाम् तेषां नास्ति कश्चिद् बले समः ।
बलदेवश्च भीमश्च मद्रराजश्च वीर्यवान् ॥
चतुर्थः कीचकस्तेषां पंचमं नानुशुश्रुम ।
अन्योन्यानंतरबलाः परस्परजयैषिणः ॥

" In the whole of the *human* world at the present day, *ncluding* the Daityas (or Negro ?), the Rakshasas (or Mongolian ?) and the Aryan races, four men, Bala-rama, Bhima, Shalya and Kichaka are the strongest, in the respective order mentioned." And in explanation of the last line, we have the *Hari-vamsha* verse which says that Bala-rama often defeated Bhima in wrestling, and gave lessons to him, as also to Duryodhana, in the art of fighting with the mace.

येन नागायुतप्राणोऽसकृद् भीमः पराजितः ।

A Puranic story, with a metaphysical and possibly also an historical and sociological significance, may be given here. The coastal island (like modern Bombay) on which Krishna founded and built his city of Dwaraka (the bulk of which was swallowed up by the sea after the passing of Krishna, and some small part only of which is said to remain now at the place known by the name of Dwaraka) was once the site of a great capital city known as Kusha-sthali, which had flourished and disappeared long ages before. A king of ancient Kusha-sthali, named Kakudmi, had a daughter named Revati. And as it has always been difficult, in all ages and all countries, to get just the right kind of husband for one's daughter, King Kakudmi suffered from that difficulty also. He thought, since one *has* to consult others about such affairs, why not go to the fountain-head at once ? And off he went, with his daughter under his arm, to Brahma, the Creator of our world-system. Now, Brahma happened to be witnessing an elaborate dancing performance given by the *apsara-s*, the light-limbed nymphs of heaven. So the king stood quiet near Brahma, as etiquette required, awaiting a convenient opportunity. One occurred shortly : an interval of rest for the dancers. He at once saluted and broached his affair. Brahma smiled graciously and said : "But while you have been watching this vast dance of the heavenly bodies for a brief minute, many aeons of human days have passed away on that very small one of these bodies, the Earth ; and your kingdom has vanished. Yet, go back quickly: Bala-rama or Sankarshana[38] (Attraction, Gravitation), who is a piece of the Maha-deva (*Ahamkara-Rudra* or *self-centered*, self-asserting egoism) principle which, in the form of the thousand-headed cyclic force called the Great Serpent Ananta, the 'endless', maintains the Earth in her proper position in the heavens, has just taken birth there, for certain special reasons concerned with the making and regulating of human history. By the time you arrive there, he will have grown up to be of marriageable age, and you will find him in a new and greater town which has sprung up on the site of your old town. He is the only atavistic human being of this terrene age who has size enough to be a good match for your daughter who belongs to the pre-historic terrene age of giants. Now, make haste." And Kakudmi rushed back with his daughter under his arm as before. But big as Bala-rama was, Revati was still a little too high. But he liked her pretty face and nice manners. So he put his

---

[38] *Samantat karshati*, who draws, attracts, from all sides; brother, and another form, of *karshati iti* Krishnah, all-attracting Beauty; the difference, apparently, being that between muscle-force, which acts from outside, and beauty-force, which acts from within, by its inherent "attractiveness".

favorite war-weapon, a huge peculiar-shaped "plough-share-and-husking-pestle"[39] on the top of the girl and she promptly telescoped down to the size he wanted. And he married her. And they were very happy ever after.

There are many astronomical cycles; one sidereal year is said to be equal to about twenty-six thousand terrene human years, and a highly advanced Individual Consciousness may be able to keep simultaneous touch with two planes of matter and two counts of time. It is also possible that Revati was a descendant of some colonisers who went off from ancient Kusha-sthali to some South Sea islands (where there still are some gigantic tribes) and happened to come to Dwaraka with her father in consequence of old traditions preserved by her tribe, in that island, and was married to Bala-rama after initiation in the ways of an agricultural civilisation—if such random speculation be permissible.

In connection with Krishna's household life—and it was a most enormous household—a comparatively little known chapter of the *Maha-bharata* (Shanti-parva, ch. 81) deserves attention, for its comic humour as well as its deep instructiveness. Says Krishna to Narada : "You are my very confidential friend, and are very learned and wise and experienced as well. Therefore I will unburden myself to you about a very secret matter. This great family and clan of mine—they call me Lord, Lord, all right enough, but in reality I am a veritable slave to them in the mask of their master. The only enjoyment allowed to me is to listen to their hard words

---

[39]The tradition is that he used to drag in his opponent with the angle of the plough-beam and the plough-share, and then knock him on the head with the huge pestle; and it was simply impossible for anyone to resist these "attractively-pounding" agricultural and domestic weapons.

and constant complaints. The incessant invective I am subjected to by those for whose welfare I am slaving, rankles in my heart perpetually. They take delight in driving the iron points of their sharp words into my soul as eagerly as the fire-maker in churning the lower piece of wood with the upper fire-stick.[40]

दास्यमैश्वर्यवादेन ज्ञातीनां वै करोम्यहम् ।
अर्धं भोक्तास्मि भोगानां वाग्दुरुक्तानि च क्षमे ॥
अरणीमग्निकामो वा मथ्नाति हृदयं मम ।
वाचा दुरुक्तं देवर्षे तन्मां दहति नित्यदा ॥
बलं संकर्षणे नित्यं सौकुमार्यं सदा गदे ।
रूपेण मत्तः प्रद्युम्नः सोऽसहायोऽस्मि नारद ॥
स्यातां यस्याहुकाक्रूरौ किन्नु दुःखतरं ततः ।
यस्य चापि न तौ स्यातां किन्नु दुःखतरं ततः ॥
सोऽहं कितवमातेव द्वयोरपि महामुने ।
एकस्य जयमाशंसे द्वितीयस्यापराजयम् ॥

[40]The inevitable fate of every public worker, on every page of history—and the nobler the worker the worse the fate! Expiation of long-past sins of previous lives—discharge of long-standing debts—this is the only explanation and great consolation. Compare the following from Emil Ludwig's fine work, *Napoleon* (pub. 1926). "At amateur theatricals, they (his brother and sister, Lucien and Elise) disport themselves in pink tights, and the Consul thunders: 'Disgraceful behavior! While I am wearing myself out trying to make people moral and respectable once more, my brother and my sister appear before the footlights almost naked!' . . All the Buonapartes exploit the man of power, that they may win money and position, lead a splendid life, and enjoy themselves, whereas in his life of superhuman toil there is little scope for pleasure" (PP. 198-199; see also 218, 222-4-5, 452, etc., for other similar instances and observations). Compare also the following passage from Nietsche, who, however, was not fortunate enough, it seems, any more than Napoleon, to possess the explanation and the consolation of the all-embracing all-charitable, all-scientific doctrines of Karma and Rebirth and Lila: "Those men who are in themselves destinies, whose advent is the advent of fate, the whole race of heroic bearers of burdens, O!, how heartily and

"My elder brother Bala-rama can think of nothing else than his muscles and his fine wines ; delicacy and fastidiousness are finished and exhausted in my younger brother Gada ; my hopeful son Pradyumna is enamored of his own pretty face ; and no one ever dreams of helping me in my endless cares and worries. Ahuka and Akrura are always quarrelling with each other, and between them I feel like the mother of two gamblers who is constantly wishing that one may win and the other not lose. I cannot do without them, and with them life is not worth living. Can you help me ?"[41]

---

gladly would they have respite from themselves for once in a while—how they crave after stout hearts and shoulders, that they might free themselves, were it but for an hour or two, from that which oppresses them! . . . At last, at last, they learn . . . to endure every body and every kind of thing . . in short, to endure still a little more than they had endured theretofore" (and to relax themselves, sometimes!).

Bear up, all good hearts! your turn of rest will come. It will come from within yourselves, by inevitable metaphysical law. After day, night. After sorrow, joy. And *vice versa*. The harder your day's work, the sounder your night's sleep. And *vice versa*! So turns the play-wheel of the world alway! The final stage of inner peace and contentment, amidst duti-ful activity as necessary, means न मोक्षस्याकांक्षा, disappearance of the *desire* for liberation, which must obviously disappear when liberation has been found. The Sufis speak of four stages, *tark-i-dunya, tark-i-uqba, tark-i-maula, tark-i-tark*, *i.e.*, renunciation of this world, of the other world, of (an external) God, and, finally, of renunciation itself.

[41] Mr. K. P. Jayaswal's work on *Hindu Polity*, published in the beginning of 1925, is a work of great learning and high value. Those interested in the uplift of India, who believe that the future cannot be solidly constructed without utilising the past, will derive valuable information from it as to the many forms of government experimented with in ancient times here. It quotes this chapter of the *Mahabharata* at length and discusses its significance in view of the republican constitution of the Andhaka-Vrshni-s. Bhishma points out (in chapter 107 of the Shanti-parva, *Mahabharata*) that

And Narada gives him this very cheerful consolation : "There are two kinds of misfortunes, Krishna ! One comes from without, and the other is created by oneself. Your misfortunes are of your own creation ! You ought to have taken the throne yourself, after slaying that tyrant Kamsa. But no, you must go and bestow it on Ahuka-Ugrasena, the doting old father of Kamsa. And now you cannot take

---

jealousies, factions, and intrigues are the main cuase of the ruin of republics. Politics become inseparably mixed up with personalities, and the party rivalries and quarrels end in the destruction of all. Compare the case of the Carthaginian and Roman oligarchies and the mediaeval Italian republics, with their perpetual conflicts between the "houses" of the "nobles". A verse of the ch.107 above referred to runs thus:

गणानां च कुलानां च राज्ञां भरतसत्तम ।
वैरसंदीपनावेतौ लोभामर्षौ नराधिप ॥

Of which, an almost literal translation, by a "curious coincidence", is the following sentence in Bryce's *Modern Democracies* (II. 591): "Oligarchies are apt to be divided into factions by the rivalries and jealousies of leading families". Another current Samskrt verse says:

सर्वे यत्र प्रणेतारः सर्वे पंडितमानिनः ।
सर्वे महत्त्वमिच्छंति तद्वृंदमाशु नश्यति ॥

"The group or party of which every member is the leader, each thinks himself to be cleverer than all the others, each wishes to become the head — such an association crumbles to pieces rapidly.

The fate of the Yadavas is illustrative. Mr. Jayaswal's discussions do not make quite clear what the exact meaning is of the words *babhru* and *bhoja* which occur in the chapter referred to in the text above (81 of the Shanti-parva of the *Maha-bharata*), as adjectives of Ugrasena (also called Ahuka) and Akrura respectively. Apparently, by inference from the circumstances, *babhru* here means a ruler or king (*Maha-bharata*, Vana, ch. 188) who decause of excessive age, or minority, or other disability is unable to perform his administrative duties himself, and *bhoja* means the regent who has to discharge them for him. The perpetual disagreements ansd quarrels and intrigues of Ugrasena and Ahuka, in conses quence of this peculiar relationship, are the main cause of Krishna's poliit back gracefully any more than a man can again eat the food he has thrown up. Your only resource now is to bear it all with patience and try to cut the tongue of invective with the soft knife that is not made of iron." "And pray what may that be?" asked Krishna. Said Narada: "Soft words in return for hard, and gifts in return for thefts; that is the only way to deal with kinsmen. No one without a great soul, without perpetual self-sacrifice, without much patient wisdom, without trusty friends, may hold together such huge clans and nations and affairs as you have undertaken, and bring them all to successful issues and prosperities. Dissension means death to a *sangha* (republic); you are the head of this *sangha*; act so that it may not break up.[42] But thou art laughing at me, my beloved Lord!, having successfully befooled the pupil into the attempt to teach his teacher and the teacher of the worlds by precept and example!"

There is much unnecessary controversy over Krishna's many wives and youthful loves. There is too much attack and too much defence. The *Bhagavata* itself raises the question and answers it.

ईश्वराणां वचः सत्यं तथैवाचरितं क्वचित् ।
धर्मव्यतिक्रमो दृष्ट ईश्वराणां च साहसम् ।

---

tico-domestic worries—for both are near relations of his also. That *babhru* means a ruler under a regency is supported by the fact that Krishna's instructions, before leaving the earth. to his faithful charioteer, Daruka, are that Babhru (though some read Vajra), the minor son of Samba, should be made chief of the remnants of the Yadavas. Apparently the republican system, of elected president, was not at all complete in that group.

[42]भेदाद् विनाशः संघानां संघमुख्योऽसि केशव ।
यथा त्वां प्राप्य नोत्सीदेदयं संघस्तथा कुरु ॥

तेजीयसां न दोषाय वह्नेः मर्वभुजो यथा ॥ and yet again,
ईश्वरैरपि भोक्नव्यं कृतं कर्म शुभाशुभं ।

" The precepts of the great are generally sound, but not so their example. They too transgress the Law and commit wilful sins. (Some say) such things are no fault in the great, the mighty ; fire can devour all things and take no harm, suffer no indigestion, (might is right. But the ultimate truth is that) the greatest have to suffer for their misdeeds as much as the smallest have to for theirs. Follow the good in their example and not the bad." "Do as I say, not as I do."[43]

In the *Taittiriya Upanishat*, the Acharya, the teacher, at the time of the *samavartana* (the University Convocation and degree-conferring ceremony of that time), says to the pupil :

यान्यस्माकं मुचरितानि तानि त्वयोपास्यानि, नो इतराणि ।

" Dear pupil ! copy in your own life only that much of our conduct which is good, and not that in it which is bad."

---

[43]Compare the following from Tolstoy's *War and Peace*, Vol.IV, Pt. III. ch. xviii: "When (their hero's) actions flagrantly contradict what humanity calls good and even right, the historians bring up the saving idea of greatness. . . . 'It is great !' say the historians, and then there is no more good or evil! *Great* is good; *not great* is bad! . . . It has never entered the mind of any man that by taking greatness as the absolute standard of good and evil, he only proclaims his own emptiness and immeasurable littleness." While the vast actions of nature-forces may be great as well as un-moral, that is , neither good nor evil, the conscious actions of human beings can never be freed from moral implications . Their great actions are either greatly good or greatly evil." The Puranas make no such mistake as is referred to by Tolstoy. They clearly say that "even Ishvara-s must reap the proper consequences of their deeds, good as well as evil," and do not admire indiscriminately. Expiations of sins by avataras have been mentioned before. Krishna's will be referred to.

Krishna's life was by no means all roses. He had and made many enemies, as every leader of men must have and make, and while he overcame most of them, he could not always have it his own way. His first-born infant son was carried away by a powerful ocean-pirate of the day, Shambara,[44] from the sea-town of Dwaraka. And Shambara kept the child successfully away from the parents, in a secure island, fostering him because of his extraordinary beauty. He gave the baby to his little daughter as a most interesting living toy. She promptly fell head over heels in love with the curious and delightful thing and doted on him. When Pradyumna grew up and came to learn the truth of his parentage from his captor-host's daughter, who also taught him all the secrets of Shambara's magic armory, he married her secretly and ran off with her on some sort of air-car (—mention of such air-cars is repeatedly made in the Puranas[45]—) and arrived in Dwaraka by his own enterprise and valor,

[44]Described as a *daitya,* or *asura,* probably belonging to some then powerful Assyrian (? Asura), Arabian, or Negro tribe. Even now the Indian Ocean and the Arabian Sea have Arabian pirates. From the poetical description of another exploit of Krishna's, *viz.,* his recovery of his teacher Sandipani's son from "the regions of the dead," it may be inferred that the boy, while bathing in the sea, at Prabhasa, was carried off by another ocean-pirate, using some sort of *sub-marine* (अंतर्जलचरः is the word used), and left on an island, or in some *southern* country, described as Yama's land (*Bhagavata,* X, ch. 45).

[45]The *Matsya Purana,* ch. 138, describes a "war in the air between the *deva-s* under Shiva and the *asura-s* under Tripura, both belligerents riding huge air-ships, over a great stretch of ocean, and a corresponding war between the sharks, in the seething waters underneath, over the corpses of the warriors as they fell from the air into the ocean, reddening its surface with the streams of blood pouring from the gaping wounds".

ईश्वरामोदिताः सर्वे उत्पेतुश्चान्तरं तदा ।
पूर्वदेवाश्च देवाश्च मूदयंतः परस्परम् ॥

after battling with and slaying the pursuing Shambara, as is the natural and regular course of events in all such episodes.

The fate of Krishna's kith and kin, and of such relatives and dependents as were left after his passing from the earth, is also very unfortunate and very sad. The end of Krishna's own body by the arrow of a fowler, who mistook a movement of his foot for that of an animal, as he sat tranced in meditation, hidden amidst shrubs near the seashore, after that awful mutual slaughter of kinsfolk, and himself withdrawing his *pranas* (vital electricities) from his body—was arranged in expiation of his slaying of Bali from a hiding-place in his previous incarnation as Rama; so say some of the Puranas. The *Padma Purana* also says that as, in the Rama-incarnation, he sided with Sugriva (son of the Sun) against his brother Bali (son of Indra) without sufficient reason, so, to make recompense, in the Krishna-incarnation he sided with Arjuna (son of Indra) against his brother Karna (son of the Sun), these two embodying, respectively, *portions* of Bali and Sugriva as well as other jiva-s, which "mystical" fact deserves pondering.

A study of the life of Krishna shows at once that it was

---

निपतन्त्यर्णवजले भीमनक्रतिमिङ्गिले ।
जग्मुस्तिमयो दैत्यान् द्रावयन्तो जलेचरान् ।।
मृधं यथासुराणां च प्रमथानां प्रवर्त्तते ।
अंबरेऽम्भसि च तथा युद्धं चक्रुर्जलेचराः ।।
यथा भ्रमति प्रमथाः सदैन्यास्तथा भ्रमन्ते तिमयः सनक्राः ।
यथैव छिन्दन्ति परस्परं तु तथैव क्रंदन्ति विभिन्नदेहाः ।।
व्रणाननैरंगरसं स्रवद्भिः सुरासुरैर्नक्रतिमिगिलैश्च ।
कृतो मुहूर्त्तेन समुद्रदेशः सरक्ततोयः समुदीर्णतोयः ।।

exceedingly rich in emotion. As there are countless shades of colours, countless tones and overtones and kinds and degrees of voices and sounds, so there are countless shades of the love-emotion (and unfortunately but inevitably, of the hate-emotion also). Every human relationship, husband, wife, father, mother, son, daughter, brother, sister, uncle, aunt, nephew, niece, grandson, granddaughter, and every one of the kinds and degrees of kinsman, relative, friend, master, servant, etc., embodies a shade, vivid or mild, of such emotion. The life of Rama by Valmiki lastingly depicts those of the more prominent relationships; different types of husband and wife, of co-wife and co-wife, of brother and brother, of parent and child, of master and servant, of teacher and pupil, of king and people, of foeman and foeman, of rival and ally, of friend and friend, of super-ordinate and sub-ordinate, of co-ordinate and co-ordinate, and so forth. But the life of Krishna as unfolded in the Puranic works and in the works of the later writers of the various schools of *bhaktas*, saintly devotees, illustrates with extraordinary richness, very many more subtle shades and grades of *bhakti*. Krishna's relations with his adoptive parents, his boy-companions, the dairymaids, his parents proper, his "college" friend Sudama, with Vyasa, Narada, Arjuna, Bhishma, with Arjuna's brothers, with his aunt Kunti, with Draupadi, with Vidura, Uddhava, Akrura, with his elder brother Bala-rama, with his different sons and daughters and grand-children, with his wives severally, Rukmini and Satya-bhama chief among them—each one of these numerous, beautiful, complex phases and aspects of the love-emotion makes subject for interesting, instructive and elevating, psychological study, and is dealt with in the literatures of the many "schools" or sects of *bhakti* which have taken birth and grown np in the subsequent centuries. His dealings with his enemies similarly illustrate his stately treatment of the hate-emotion. When he goes to Dhrta-rashtra, as ambassador of the Pandavas, to make a last vain effort to ward off war, Duryodhana invites him to be his guest. He declines.

संप्रीतिभोज्यान्यन्नानि आपद्भोज्यानि वा पुनः ।
न च त्वं प्रीयसे राजन् न चैवापद्गता वयम् ॥

"The bread offered by loving friendship may be eaten, O king! or the bread brought by misfortune. Thou bearest us no love, and we are not stricken by misfortune!"[46] And he goes uninvited to Vidura's house and stays there, for Vidura loves him. Krishna offers boons to Vidura at

---

[46]This verse offers an illuminating commentary on the present-day ossification of caste into mere sheer mominal heredity and rabid touch-me-not-ism in food and drink, not on the ground of rational cleanliness, but only of difference of name of caste or sub-caste—which constitutes the one poison that is slowly killing Hinduism now. There is nothing in *Manu-smrti*–the foundation of Sanatana Dharma (commonly known as Hinduism )—to justify this utterly senseless and reasonless arrogance-promoting, sympathy-killing, hate-creating, touch-me-not-ism. There is much to justify the opposite. There is also much in it to show that caste is not only and purely hereditary and unchangeable.

The Veda (Atharva) expressly says:

समानी प्रपा सह वो अन्नभागः समाने योक्त्रे सह वो युनज्मि ।

"Drink water together, share your food together; in the same bond of affection and co-operation for all good works I bind you all together." And Sayana comments on this:

"Because of mutual affection, you should eat and drink together in the same place or from the same dish." But the modern self-righteous Hindu's greatest boast is that he does not take even any drinking water touched by another! What wonder that he is being laughed at and trampled upon. Dining together inpliess sympathy, friendship, intimacy, ordinarily. Avoiding it implies the opposite, strangeness, distrust, antipathy, ordinarily. And the house divided against itself will fall.

parting and the dear old gentleman asks this boon: "May there always be affection between thee and me, and may my house never lack worthy guests and lots of roly-poly babies and plenty of nice things for them all to eat!"

अस्तु मे त्वयि रतिः सुताकुलं भोज्यमप्यतिथिसंकुलं कुलम् ॥

Krishna's deferential treatment of those elders who, for special reasons, fought *against* him and his dear friends, the Pandavas, in the great war, but loved and honored him and them all the same, and wished them victory all the time—is another great lesson in that deliberately dramatic manner of high chivalry in which great and advanced souls treat the tragi-comedy of this world's procession of events.

The Samskrt Science of Rhetoric says that "emotional enjoyment is the soul or essence of poetry," and, indeed, of all fine art; and it subdivides this enjoyment, *rasa*, "taste," "unction," into nine principal kinds of motifs or interests. The *Bhagavata* loves to show that Krishna, as a theme for poetry, exhausted all these in himself. The occasion is the then very young Krishna's entry into the arena of the tournament which had been planned by Kamsa in a last effort to murder him, but at which he himself was slain by Krishna. Krishna enters, carrying on one shoulder a great tusk torn from the elephant Kuvalayapida, which had been stationed at the gateway to kill Krishna, but which had been killed by him. "To the gladiators pitted against him, he appeared *Fierce* and *Furious* as the thunderbolt of heaven; to the masculine spectators, as *Wonderful* specimen of perfect manhood; to the women, as the *Beautiful* Eros incarnate; to the cowherds, as playmate full of *Laughter* and *Fun*; to the bad and ferocious but valorous kings assembled there, as *Heroic* chastiser of the wicked; to his parents, also present there, as precious child, object of tender *Compassion;* to Kamsa, as the *Terrible* Lord of Death himself; to the shallow-minded, as *Disgustingly* stained with the stains of battle; to the *yogis*, as the embodiment of the *Peace* of the Universal Self, the eternal object of single-minded *Devotion;* and as their idolised personal deity, the focus of their whole-hearted *affection*, to his kinsfolk of the Vrshni clan."

मल्लानामशनिर्नृणां नरवर: स्त्रीणां स्मरो मूर्त्तिमान्
गोपानां स्वजनोऽसतां क्षितिभुजां शास्ता स्वपित्रो: शिशु: ।
मृत्युर्भोजपतेर्विराडविदुषां तत्त्वं परं योगिनां
वृष्णीनां परदेवतेति विदितो रंगं गत: केशव: ॥

*Bhagavata*

रौद्रोऽद्भुतश्च शृङ्गारो हास्यो वीरं दया तथा ।
भयानकश्च बीभत्स: शान्त: सप्रेमभक्तिक: ॥

Shridhara's *Tika* on the above.

What wonder that Krishna, image in miniature of the Great Self, the One Playwright of the World-Process, should treat life deliberately as drama to be enjoyed by the consummate artist that he was. To create objects and situations for the purpose of *enjoying* them, *tasting* them leisurely, is art. The compiler of the Book of Genesis realised this when he recorded that God, after having made the world, looked at it and said: "It is good." His enjoying it thus proves that He carries on this World-Process as the Supreme Artist, "Kavi" as the Upanishats say.

## THE EUGENIC VALUE OF KRISHNA-WORSHIP

It is obvious that the Krishna-avatara was not immaculate like the Rama-avatara; but, at the same time, there is clear indication in the *Bhagavata* that what are called

Krishna's youthful loves did not go beyond violent flirtations, and a taste for group-dancing and singing, like the waltzes and quadrilles and fandangos and maypoles of the West, and the *kajli* and the *kolattam* of the northern and southern India of to-day. One of his many names and epithets, *viz.*, Achyuta, signifies "the chaste," "the continent." And the *Bhagavata* (III, ii, 26) says that " he lived in the home of his adoptive father Nanda, tending cows, stealing butter, romping with girls, and battling with wild animals, till only the eleventh year of his life," going off to Mathura then, and afterwards thence to Dwaraka.

नतो नन्दव्रजं नीतः पित्रा कंसाद् विबिभ्यता ।
एकादशसमास्तत्र गूढार्चिः सबलोऽवसत् ॥

If this be so, then his dancings and firtings show nothing seriously wrong, but rather only a precocious manifestation, even in early boy-hood, of another aspect of Krishna's richly artistic and vital nature; and in any case, he was correct and proper after his marriage,[47] though that, of course, was very manifold—but that was in accordance with the then custom.

---

[47]Not quite, though, unfortunately. If he had rested content with his eight wives he might have been saved many domestic worries. In one of his chivalrous expeditions to succour the oppressed and break the militarist, he went so far east as the present Assam, and slew Bhauma, the Rakshasa-king, and set free "sixteen thousand" maidens this time (as it was "kings" or nobles, in the expedition against Jarasandha). All the maidens, of course, promptly fell in love with their rescuer, who was also the handsomest man of his day, if not of all times, besides: and he, in a thoughtless moment, accepted this very voluminous love; though mystical causes, belonging to previous births, are also assigned. Some Puranas mention, with reaslistic touch, various domestic scandals, as the consequence of the immense size of this household, in which Krishna's son Samba was concerned, and the curse inflicted on the youth, and his

After leaving Vrnda-vana for Dwaraka, Krishna "turned over a new leaf," in modern colloquial phrase. He never returned to it again, although he had promised to the dairymaids that he would, shortly. This truant lover's promise he fulfilled vicariously, however, through his dear friend and pupil Uddhava.[48] That he did fulfil it thus and send much loving endearment and consolation and advice to the overfond girl-playmates of his boyhood, only shows his kind softness of heart, his recognition of responsibility, his wish to help and make amends. The "Bee-song," by Sur Das, of the maids' complaints to Uddhava, is one of the finest pieces of work in Hindi poetry. The revival of Vrnda-vana by Chaitanya in the fifteenth century is the latest "return of Krishna" to it, after the devastation of the sister-town of Mathura by Mahmud of Ghazni in A. D. 1018,

---

illness and cure by Sun-worship and sun-bath. After Krishna's passing, as Arjuna, stunned by misery at the loss of Krishna, was convoying this vast crowd to Indra-prastha (Delhi), robbers fell upon the procession, and the irresistible warrior, now faint with sorrow, was unable to beat them off, and they carried away many, and "many of the women went away of their own accord with the robbers," says the *Maha-bharata*, Mausala-parva, ch. 8. Sixteen thousand may be an exaggeration, but even some recent "ruling" chiefs of India have been "credited" by popular rumor with harems of so many as four thousand. Some of the Roman and the Persian Emperors, were not very far behind, it seems. The primal appetites of tongue and sex, in wrong use, bring the greatest ills upon mankind: in right use, the greatest joys.

[48] One or two Puranas make him redeem the promise personally; others say he met the girl-friends of his boyhood, later on in life, not in Vrnda-vana, but at another place of pilgrimage, to which both happened to have travelled for some holy-day. The anciency of Krishna-worship is attested from time to time by antiquarian finds, like those of the monolithic column dedicated to Vasudeva, at Besnagar near Bhilsa in Central India, by a Greek envoy named Heliodoros, which scholars date between 140 and 130 B.C.

when it is said to have "contained nearly ten thousand temples," the finest of which, in the centre of the city, is described by Mahmud himself thus: "If anyone should undertake to build a fabric like that, he would have to expend thereon one hundred thousand packets of a thousand dinars and would not complete it in two hundred years with the assistance of the most ingenious masters."[49] Yet he destroyed it !

Instead of vainly carping at his ways, and warping our own artistic faculties and potencies thereby, we ought to take from Krishna's exuberant and overflowing stores of all that is beautiful and joyous, as much as we can assimilate lawfully, for the purpose of enriching and refining our own emotional life and capacities, adding a many-sided flavor to our domesticity, and thereby helping ourselves to realise an essential part of the first purpose of life, mentioned before.

---

[49]See p. 74, Vol. III of C. V. Vaidya's *History of Medieval India*, a very valuable work. Naturally the first words that spring to the lips when one pictures all the architectural beauty thus destroyed are: "What a brutal and savage marauder!" But thinking deeper, one senses the psychical corruption that had begun to fester underneath the artistic surface, and deservedly brought upon itself "the scourge of God". The scourge was no doubt a brutal marauder, but the scourged deserved him. Yet, if these "scourges" had destroyed only the ugly and preserved the beautiful, how different would the inhabited places of the Earth have been to-day!

Why could they not leave the beautiful buildings intact and content themselves with taking away the movable wealth that was stored in such temples, for much the same purpose, probably (at least in original intention, though the priesthood began misappropriating it later), as war-spoils were in old Rome in the temple of Saturn, *viz.*, for public use in times of dire calamity, famines, foreign invasions, etc.!

धर्माविरुद्धो भूतेषु कामोऽस्मि भरतर्षभ ॥ *Gita, VII,* 11

बिभ्रद्वपुः सकलसुंदरसंनिवेशं
कर्माचरन् भुवि सुमंगलमाप्तकामः ।
कृत्वा निमित्तमितरेतरतः समेतान्
हत्वा नृपान् निरहरत् क्षितिभारमीशः ॥

*Bhagavata, XI, i,* 2–10

"The oneness of the I manifests as the desire for oneness, for union, *i.e.*, as the lawful loves of men and women, O Arjuna!" "Krishna came to irradiate the life of this earth with the splendor of his physical vesture, wherein were gathered and concentrated the finest essences of all things that are most beautiful; so perfectly fulfilled was he in himself that he wanted nothing outside of himself, yet did he continuously discharge human duties and do acts of piety and merit for the instruction of others by his great example; wielding the kings of the earth as his playthings, he destroyed them by one another, in order to lighten the burden of the Earth."

Truly, if sunsets and sunrises, if cloud and sea and snow-peak, if moon and star and bird and flower are worth looking upon, if we may without sin admire a fine horse, a beautiful mare, a magnificent tusker, a sleek and gentle milch-cow, a grand bull, why may we not admire far more, a beautiful human face and figure ? But it ought to be admired *in the same spirit*, as a work of Nature's supreme art. For this purpose public opinion has to be carefully educated. There is too much license on the one side and too much puritanism on the other. If the proper wise middle course were followed there would be more joy in life, and there would be more human faces and features *worth* admiring and looking at again and again. For in the biological and psychological worlds, as in the economic, supply follows demand, and a whole nation's appreciation of and craving for physical, mental, and moral beauty, necessarily *creates* more and more of such beauty in each of its successive generations. The worship, by brides and bridegrooms, of Krishna as baby, as boy, as youth, and as great man, charming, fascinating, piquant, saucy, mischievous, wilful, maddeningly beautiful. hero of heroes, aesthete of aesthetes, teacher of teachers, grand in every respect, has its own most beneficent eugenic value for the nation, *if the worship be only duly intelligent*, and guided by just and righteous and wise elders; and not by knaves and hypocrites as it is so largely to-day, to the shame and the sorrow of the people. The worship of "heroes," and of "mother and child"–Gauri and Ganesha, Kausalya and Rama, Yashoda and Krishna, Isis and Horus, Yashodhara and Rahula, Venus and Cupid, Kwánnon and Baby, Mary and Jesus, Fatima and Hasan-Husain—in all religions, should, but does not, serve the same purpose. The *Vasant-otsava*, or "the spring-festival," with its *Holika-daha* (bonfires to burn up the accumulated rubbish of the winter and make a general spring-cleaning) and its worship of the Chatuh-Shashti Devi (the "goddess of the sixty-four fine arts" which subserve refined *Kama*-enjoyment), has similarly degenerated in modern India. The shell of the custom remains, the spirit has vanished. The refinements have gone, the coarsenesses have become accentuated. From being a festival of delicate refinements and artistic enjoyments, it has become a carnival of indecent songs and conduct. It is matter for regretful surprise that the highly intelligent and scientific nations of the West should also have failed so far to profit by their researches in the ancient Greek cult of Beauty, and to initiate and pursue more systematic methods for their own physical improvement.[50]

Incidentally, our younger generation may usefully make a careful study of the sizes and qualities of the physical bodies that the great men of history have worn.

Few great men of action, though some of thought and of art, have been puny or sickly or ill-formed and feeble. They have generally carefully educated and strengthened their bodies at least as much as their minds. And to the youth of India, the example of Krishna and his compatriots is a shining light. The students in the higher classes might, with much profit, also study something of the birth-conditions and the personal habits and private life of the prominent figures of history. Ab-normal, *i.e.*, extra-ordinary, personages often have extraordinary birth-conditions, and these and their personal habits and conduct in respect of dietary and sex-life throw a most valuable light on their achievements or failures.[51] The Purana-Itihasa are perhaps more "scientific" in this respect than many modern text-books and, *if properly interpreted*, are seen to embody an "historical sense" which is finer, deeper-rooted, and more comprehensive and scientific and philosophical.[52] They are honored as "the fifth Veda," by tradition.

---

[50]Schools of Physical Culture seem to be multiplying now in the West, however.

[51]"Tell me what a man eats and I will tell you what he is"–is a remark made by a Frenchman, Brillat-Savarin.

[52]Unfortunately, there is little doubt that the current texts are full of misreadings and interpolations; and at the same time, it is very difficult to determine the right wording and nail down the interpolations. Also, there is a lot of "mystical " matter in them which, on the one hand, is not easy to throw away as rubbish, in view of its elaborate nature, and,

इतिहासपुराणं च पंचमं वेदानां वेदं भगवोऽध्येमि ।

*Chhandogya-Upanishat.*

And Manu enjoins: "The Sciences should be studied in the light of History, *Itihasa*, the History of the Human Race, in detail, and *Purana*, the History of the Solar System as a whole, generally; since, without the help of these, which supply the concrete illustrations of abstract principles, the true meaning of those sciences cannot be realised."

Incidentally also it may be mentioned here, for the information of those who are inclined to see more vice than virtue in Krishna, that the private morals of such historical figures as Julius Caesar and Alexander and Napoleon were worse (because adulterous), and even Aristotle sometimes joined in his pupil Alexander's revels. But despite all such weaknesses, which no doubt had bad effects on their work in life, we cannot but admire their great achievements. We ought to understand and recognise the strong points as well as weak points, the good as well as the evil.

विद्वान् गुणज्ञो दोषज्ञः ।

"The wise man understands the virtues as well as the defects of things and persons." Some ill-advised and narrow-thinking Christian missionaries, misconceiving their duty to their own great Master, a true "son of God," *i.e.*, an avatara in his own degree, think that they serve the Christ by slandering Krishna.[53] If they came face to face with

on the other, is even more difficult to interpret satisfactorily. in the absence of "superphysical" knowledge.

[53]Apparently in Christian Mysticism, the expression "Son of God" (as in I John, III, 2-3, "Beloved, now are we children of God, etc.") stands for the *Jivan-mukta* or *purna-purusha* of Vedanta, and the *insan-ul-kamil*, the "perfect man," of Sufism.

their Master, surely he would rebuke them greatly, The Christ cannot be exalted by the belittlement of Krishna. Different manifestations of God, for different purposes, have to be reverently studied from different points of view; they cannot all be measured off, offhand, by the same foot-rule.

## KRISHNA AND CHRIST

From other and more generous points of view, parallels have now and then been attempted between the lives of Krishna and Christ. But they are very far-fetched. If we take a few selected incidents from each life, similarities may no doubt be found, especially if we follow those who think that the Biblical Christ is not an historical person, that Jesus was born 105 B.C. or so, and that Krishna also is a myth—the selected incidents being similar because they allegorise the same spiritual truths. But, then, for the purposes of the inner science, the birth, growth, struggles, decay, death, of a little plant, a worm, a man, *all equally* allegorise the one truth of all truths, *viz.*, the cyclic descent of Spirit into Matter and its reascent thereout. Apart from this, and regarded as historical, the two lives are different as different can be. There is very little in common between the gentle ministry of the Christ, extending over only three years out of the thirty-three of his life, and the tremendous all-comprehending activity of Krishna, throughout a very long life of the fullest and intensest kind. The one was essentially a soul-refining force, the other was that, and an immediate history-maker on a very large scale, and a philosophical and artistic teacher of the highest order, besides. Both taught, but the teaching was directed to different purposes. The former taught "Resist not evil, Turn the right cheek," the latter "Therefore fight". And yet the two teachings are entirely in accord. For the former means "when the wrong is done to yourself," and the latter "when the wrong is done to another who is dependent on you for protection".[54] Jesus taught: "Love thine enemies, love thy neighbor as thyself, love God with all thy heart." Krishna adds the luminous reason: " Because the Essence of all is the universal common Self". The former deals more with the individual in and by himself: the latter, more with the individual as a member of a community. As has been observed by some writers, while some reformers seek to reform human nature, others seek to reform human institutions: but Manu and, following him, Krishna do both, by laying down the just lines of that greatest of human institutions, a right organisation of society as a whole, and then pointing out the duty of each individual member thereof in keeping with his special position therein.

The general conditions, of the prevailing of *a-dharma* (sin) over *dharma* (virtue), in matters social, political, economical, amidst which the Christ arose and worked, were different from those amidst which Krishna arose and worked. The Christ strove to reform, by teaching and arousing, through precept and example, internal, subjective, individual intensity of *feeling*, of faith, hope, charity, self-purification, and devotion to the Father in Heaven (*Savita Devah*

---

[54] At the same time it should be noted that turning the cheek—but *en masse*—is one of the most effective forms of fighting. Non-violent non-co-operation, passive resistance, (not acquiescence but *resistance*, though *passive*), civil disobedience, general strike, "suffering wrong but not doing it," *hartal*, *hijrat*, are all only different forms and degrees of the manifestation of this "Soul-force," which, it may be observed in passing, is stronger in the woman-nature than in the man-nature.

of the Gayatri) —all culminating in self-sacrifice. Krishna taught utmost self-sacrifice also, but as culmination of inner illumination, of *knowledge* of the Universal Self, and of the sense of duty born of that knowledge; and he strove to reform by external, objective adjustments of human affairs, by rewards and punishments, on an immense scale also. Christ taught *bhakti* to the Universal Father, and inspired personal devotion to himself; Krishna taught *jnana* of the Universal Self and. as the consequence of that, Universal Love, and he inspired intense personal devotion also.[55]

### The Rationale of Ideals

More might be said of the devotion inspired by Krishna. But for that it is better to go to the great classical works direct, and to the *Bhagavata* more than any other work. Like all other men of action, and more than they in the degree of his greatness, Krishna inspired violent dislikes as well as likes. But the all-charitable, all-helping, ancient Science of the Spirit says that those who hated Krishna were as much helped in their soul-development as those who loved him. This seems to be a mystic mystery. But it is far from being unintelligible. It is explained by superphysical science, which tells us that, just as in the physical world, patriarchs and their families, chiefs and their clans and tribes, elders

[55]Of course. the ultimate metaphysical teaching of all these great teachers is the same. Christ also said: "I and my Father are One." "Ye are the living temples of God." And Muhammad says in the Quran : "Inni an-Allahu, la ilaha illa Ana." which is an exact translation of Isaiah : "Verily, I, even I am (is) God, and there is none else." The verses in Ecclesiastes (iv.8, 9) are very remarkable, too: "There is One alone, and there is not a second," "Two are better than one." (Cf: Brhad., I. iv. 1-3).

and their communities and nations, stand in special relations of protectiveness and loyalty towards one another, even so specially advanced souls, *Ishvaras*, stand in special relations of compassion, to help them along the path of psycho-physical evolution, with large groups of souls. As the *Yoga-bhashya* indicates, the Ishvara suffers from that noblest and most refined Avidya, nescience, that Divine Heartache, Moha, Klesha, of the Buddhas of Compassion, which makes Him say: "I will take these erring souls to safety, across the vast abysms of Kalpa-pralayas and Maha-pralayas, by teaching them the Eternal Truth of the Immortal Self and Its laws." It is this purest form of Maya which makes Him retain a *material* sheath, however glorious and subtle, *Dharma-kaya*, etc., and provides Him with motive for, and interest in, existence.

It is, otherwise also, plain psychology. Thus.

Narada says to Yudhishthira that when the object is truly great, it does not matter whether the bond with which you tie your soul to it is the bond of some form of the hate-emotion or some form of the love-emotion. The result will be good for you either way. It is enough that you *tie* yourself strongly to this great soul. But make sure that he *is* truly great and not a hollow pretender. He will do the rest. Of course you will have more pain along the one way than along the other. But dragged you will be, either way, to the right goal. The way of sin and pain may be even quicker, for life thereon is more intense, more "fast", and wears out the emotion-bonds that tie to the earth, more quickly, by very powerful revulsion. Jaya and Vijaya, offered the option between *three* births as foes of Vishnu, or *seven* as devotees, chose the former, and took birth as

(1) Hiranyaksha and Hiranya-kashipu, (2) Ravana and Kumbhakarna, (3) Shishu-pala and Danta-vaktra. He who wrestles with God touches, catches, embraces Him more closely and more vigorously than he who worships Him, awe-struck, from a distance. Arjuna wrestled with Shiva and received the Pashupat-astra, the irresistible weapon. Jacob wrestled with the angel. The soul *seeking* God, first denies Him angrily, then becomes God, Itself.

गोप्यः कामाद् भयात्कंसो द्वेषाच्चैद्यादयो नृपाः ।
संबंधाद् वृष्णयो यूयं मख्याद् भक्त्या वयं विभो ॥

*Bhagavata*

"By sex-love, by fear, by hate, by kinsmanship, by deep friendship, by whole-hearted devotion, have different souls clung to Him, and found Him."[56]

In this way has Krishna received a devoted worship which flourishes five thousand years after his passing with an intensity unsurpassed in any time or clime.

Of course the deepest reason of such denouement is *in the soul of the votary himself*, the soul which makes the ideal

[56]See how, in common history, the favorite valets and horses and weapons of the "great" share in the "immortality" of the masters whom they have served devotedly and well. Alexander's Bucephalus and Napoleon's Rustam and Arthur's Excalibur are as well known as their masters. Krishna's *chakra* (discus) Sudarshana, his bow Sharnga, his chrioteer Daruka, his four horses Shaibya, etc., his pauper "school-mate" Sudama, and his boyhood's dairyfriends, Radha Lalita, etc., are inseparable from his great story. The fifth principle, if it will only attach itself firmly enough to the sixth, will, without fail, partake of the latter's immortality.

object of its clinging a means for its own psychical exercise and strengthening.

> यत्र यत्र मनो देही धारयेत् सकलं धिया ।
> स्नेहाद् द्वेषाद् भयाद् वापि याति तत्तत्स्वरूपताम् ॥

*Bhagavata*

> चित्तमेव हि संसारस्तत्प्रयत्नेन शोधयेत् ।
> यच्चित्तस्तन्मयो भवति गुह्यमेतत्सनातनम् ॥

*Maitrayani-Upanishat*

> यं यं वापि स्मरन् भावं त्यजत्यन्ते कलेवरम् ।
> तं तमेवैति कौंतेय सदा तद्भावभावितः ॥
> श्रद्धामयोऽयं पुरुषः यो यच्छ्रद्धः स एव सः ॥ *Gita*

"Whatsoever the embodied *jiva* puts its mind, its heart, into; whatsoever ideal, whatsoever object of desire, it dwells upon, single-mindedly, whole-heartedly, whether by love, or by hate, or by fear—it puts on the form of, it becomes, that same ideal or object. The world-procession *is* mind; purify the mind therefore with all thy might; for the man becomes what he has in mind; especially when leaving the body at its death. The man *is* his wish, his aspiration."

In the words of western poets,

> "Whatsoever thou lovest, that become thou must,
> God if thou love God, dust if thou love dust."
> "Evil is the thought that thinks it,
> Good the thought that makes it so.
> Light and Darkness, Sin and Pureness,
> Likewise out of thinking grow.
> Dwell in thought upon the Grandest,

And the Grandest you shall be.
Fix your thought upon the Highest,
And the Highest you shall be."

The *mind* verily creates, and *is*, the world.

## Krishna as Master of Superphysical Powers

The *Shakta Agama* says that the human *jiva* passes through three stages in evolution: (1) the *pashu* or "animal" -man; (2) the *vira* or "hero" -man; (3) the *divya* or "god" -man.[57] The divine man, the superman, has superphysical powers, subtle sensor and motor faculties with reaches beyond the "hero's". These are either congenital (and persons born with such extraordinary faculties are said to belong to the *rshi*-class of *jiva*[58]), or are developed by special exercises and experiences of *tapasya* (ascetic practices) and *yoga*[59] in this life. If they have been worked at in previous lives, they appear congenitally in this, or, in any case, their revival or further development becomes easier; for all faculties or powers are already present in the Self, and therefore in every self or *jiva*, but the manifestation of any and every one of them is matter of perfection of, and adjustment and

---

[57]Compare (1) the *Insan-ul-haiwani* (the animal-man) : (2) the *Insan* (ordinary man); and (3) the *Insan-ul-kamil* the perfect man) -of Sufism.

[58]Compare the saying: नार्वाचीनेषु ऋषयो जायंते· "*rshi-s* are not born among the latter-day degenerates": or, ऋषीणां च नदीनां च जन्मस्थानं न लक्ष्यते, "the birth-place of *rshi-s*, as of rivers, is not easy to ascertain." Many grades of *rshi-s* and *munis* are distinguished (as *nabi, auliya, etc.*, in Sufism). The presence of some abnormal powers of second-sight, etc.. without high intellectual development and moral qualities, may be found among degenerates and savages also, sometimes. To make the *rshi*, high moral and intellectual as well as superphysical qualities are needed .

[59]The Sufi word for *yoga* is *suluk*.

co-ordination between, the subtler (*karana* and *sukshma*) bodies, which the *jiva* brings over from the "other worlds," and the physical dense (*sthula*) body which it finds here.

Of course, the "great soul," going to incarnate on the earth for a special purpose, seeks out the family, and therein the parents, most favorably constituted psycho-physically for its requirements. But, from the nature of things, *rshi*-families cannot be common, or even frequent, in a human race which is so defective and overpowered by *a-dharma* (sin) as to need an avatara to uplift it into *dharma* (virtue) again. At the same time, a *human* race can, ordinarily, be helped properly only by one who is *human* as well as superhuman. And it happens also that Nature is made up of opposites, *dvam-dvam*, twos and twos, though only one of a pair predominates at any given time and place. Therefore when *a-dharma* prevails, *dharma* is not, cannot be. wholly destroyed but is focussed, necessarily, into powerful "seeds" here and there, from which its great "banyan-trees" (*ashvattha*) must arise again to spread their branches over the world. Thus, in times of great and widespread lawlessness, disorder, and sin, *dharma* and wisdom and physical and superphysical powers become concentrated in families here and there in potentiality. And the finest-grained physical body available in such, with reference to its requirements, is taken by the great soul to begin with; though there are violent exceptions also, and saints are sometimes born in a family of sinners, like embodiments of its conscience, for there is a duality, an ambivalence, an opposition of pairs, in a family, as in an individual, and in a community, a "bundle of contradictions," elements of good and elements of evil. Prahlada was born as son to Hiranya-kashipu, and Vibhishana as brother to Ravana. Yet the body also always needs to be further trained and perfected up to those requirements, by special baptism, initiation, vows, fasts, vigils, periods of retirement from the busy haunts of men, ascetic austerities, solitary meditations, trances, wrestlings with angels and with devils (inner and outer), communion with beings of other worlds, with Nature, with Cosmic Life and Consciousness.[60]

We therefore generally find periods of such retirement and ascetic practices, of the restraints of the outer sensor and motor organs, which dam back psychic energy, and force it to enter into, and develop, the germs of the inner, and consequent extensions of faculty, and mystical experiences of various kinds and degrees, in the lives of almost all extra-ordinarily great men.[61] The biography of Krishna contains many periods of intense *tapasya* and meditation, deliberately undergone for further perfecting of his "vehicles," over and above the specially favorable conditions secured by the captivity of his parents, their consequent high-strung nervous psycho-physical condition, their intensely prayerful mood, and their longing for the foretold birth of one who would deliver not only them but the whole

---

[60] उपनयन, दीक्षा, व्रत, उपवास, जागरण, एकांतवास, तपस्या, ऋषि-चर्या, संयम, ध्यान, धारणा, समाधि, अंतरायजय, सिद्धदर्शन, देवसंगम, आत्मलाभ.

Compare the practices known under the name of *Suluk* in Sufism. ब्रह्मानंद is called by the Sufis *lazzat-ul-ilahiya*. ब्रह्मलीनता or ब्रह्मभाव is *ittihad* or *wisal* or *jam*, Nirvana is *Fana-fi-llah*. annihilation into God, mergence into the Universal Life.

[61] Compare the cases of Christ and Muhammad.

world, and not only from physical and political bondage to tyrants, but also from spiritual bondage to a degenerated priesthood and a superstitious pseudo-religion. It may be noted that these parents were themselves reincarnations of the primeval *rshi-s*, Kashyapa and Aditi, to whom Vishnu-Krishna or Narayana was born as Upendra Vamana; and of the still earlier *rshi-s* Sutapa and Prshni, to whom he was born as Prshni-garbha, according to the Puranas. By such *tapasya* Krishna further refined and perfected his already gloriously splendid body into a fit instrument for the manifestation of marvellous superphysical as well as physical powers.[62]

We may note that while the *rshi* is, ordinarily, a man of thought, a teacher, and therefore does not need much physical muscular vigor, Krishna had to work pre-eminently as both man of thought and of action. Hence his need for exceptional superphysical as well as exceptional physical body, in keeping with his exceptional greatness as avataric-*jiva*, "a hair from the head of Narayana," "a ray of the Sun-centre". He gave illuminating visions to his parents, his nurse-mother Yashoda, and his friends Arjuna and Narada. He gave terror-striking visions to the evil-minded Duryodhana and others. He saw from Dwaraka, a thousand miles away, Draupadi's agony of shame, and heard her cry to him for help, in Hastinapur, when Dus-shasana, at the bidding of his elder brother Duryodhana, who had won

---

[62]There are sects, as in the case of Christ, which believe, respectively, in Krishna's "immaculate conception." and in his possessing a body made up, not of the "common elements." but of ethereal stuff–yet the "common " is miraculous enough!

her from Yudhishthira in that mad game of dice, endeavored to pull away her cloth and denude her as a slave, in the assembly-hall;[63] and he answered the cry also, and, across all that distance, either hypnotised Dus-shasana and the whole assembly into "seeing" her cloth stretch exhaustlessly, or actually "multiplied" and lengthened it endlessly (as the books say), by instantaneous materialisation. He also "multiplied" the minute remains of the food cooked by Draupadi, in order to enable her to feed and mollify the very choleric and curse-ful *rshi* Durvasa and his many disciples, (as the Christ, later, multiplied the loaves and fishes). He projected his own and also his beloved friend Arjuna's *sukshma-sharira-s* (subtle bodies ) on certain occasions of profound disturbance of mind and intensity of emotion. He appeared simultaneously in many places on other occasions. He healed the sick and straightened the deformed by the radiant vital magnetism which made his caressing touch pour health

[63]It seems that, as later among the "civilised" Romans, there were women-slaves as well as men-slaves in India in those days; and that they were kept more or less bare-bodied; but not wholly so as in some periods of Rome. There does not seem to be any mention of such utter nudity of slaves in India, in the old books. But, even so, it is quite evident, through all the glamor of Vyasa's grand Samskrt, that, together with a very high development of all kinds of arts and luxuries and weapons of warfare, there was much coarse living and sensual and even brutal indulgence, in those days, drinking and dicing and lusting, even as today in the great capital-towns of the West and the East; with apparently this difference that the brutality was more frank and openly recognised by convention in those days, while nowadays it is more covered with films of decorum and is mostly confined to "the night-side" of the great cities. The *yaksha-s* and *raksha-s*, evil microbes, disease-germs, evil passions, fiends and hobgoblins,and beasts of prey—all grow more powerful in the dark, when the Sun's rays, "angels," *deva-s*, are not fighting with and destroying or at least checking and suppressing them.

into the ill and make them whole, and fill with blissful intoxication the already whole who had the rare fortune to be near and dear to him. He also, on rare occasions, brought back the dead to life, where apparently, the link between the subtle and the dense bodies had not been wholly broken, by that same magnetic power and will-force. He laid dooms upon specially grievous sinners, as of prolonged wandering in spiritual and physical misery upon Ashvatthama, the killer of infants and sleepers.[64] Such things are said of him by written and spoken tradition, and naturally and justly belong to him as a superman. Many more things are also said of him which extend his greatness and his glory beyond all bounds, and make of him a very god on earth. How far they are due to poetical license and exaltation, or devotional and sentimental exaggeration, or mixture of fact with fantasy, it is difficult to say. But reason counsels some proportion with other great figures and events of history and facts of Nature.

His mastery of martial weapons, whether "secret" *astra-s*, or plain *shastra-s*[65] like the bow and arrow, the mace, the sword, and his special favorite, the *chakra* or discus,[66] need not be particularly dwelt on in this connection. That mastery, no doubt, was personal and unique, and outdistanced even Arjuna's and Bhishma's and Drona's. Still, it does not seem

[64] Compare the legend of the curse laid by Jesus on the Wandering Jew.

[65] *Astra*, from *as*, *asyate*, "is flung from a distance"; *shastra*. from *shas*, *shasati*, "cuts up, cleaves into pieces."

[66] It seems to have been in use in India to the end of the seventh century A.D. The Arab invaders of Sind, of that time, have recorded that, flung by the Indian warriors, it could completely cut through the neck of a horse, severing the head. (*Vide* C. V. Vaidya's *Medieval India.*)

to have been specially connected with any superphysical quality, for the use of such "secret" *astra-s* was common to all the *maha-rathas*, the great warrior-heroes, the "chivalrous knights," of that day. The recent lethal inventions of Europe for purposes of war make the Puranic *astra-s* look less hyperbolical than they formerly did. They seem to have been specially prepared "flinging" weapons, with much power of destruction, the secret of the use of which was imparted only to the select.

### Krishna as Man of Knowledge and Teacher

Finally we may see Krishna as one of the greatest of teachers.

While his beauty of form remains only as a tradition, and alas, there is no authentic portrait available either on canvas or in marble, no true *chitra* or *pratima*, to show us concretely what that marvel was like; while his deeds remain only in results long overlaid and modified by the results of other events, brought on by the unresting stream of time, moving now peacefully and placidly and now torrentially; the wisdom of his teachings remains to us in direct form. Even in his boyhood and youth he was a zealous reformer of religion. He battled bravely as a boy, against the prevalent excessive and sensuous (or when perversely misinterpreted then even positively corrupting) Vedic formalism and ritualism; warred upon vested priestly or rather priestcrafty interests and pretensions; successfully abolished the Indra-*makha* with its blood-sacrifices and libations and potations; and established, instead, the more rational cult of the cow, so eminently suited to an agricultural civilisation. This open condemnation of hypocritical, cunning, selfish and senseless, or perverse and depraved sacerdotal formalism, and of the endeavor to hypnotise the people with the mere outer word of the Veda, is briefly but strongly repeated by him in his later teaching of the *Gita*.

### Ritualism *vs.* Wisdom

यामिमां पुष्पितां वाचं प्रवदन्त्यविपश्चितः ।
वेदवादरताः पार्थ नान्यदस्तीति वादिनः ॥
कामात्मानः स्वर्गपरा जन्मकर्मफलप्रदाम् ।
क्रियाविशेषबहुलां भोगैश्वर्यगतिं प्रति ॥
भोगैश्वर्यप्रसक्तानां तयाऽपहृतचेतसाम् ।
व्यवसायात्मिका बुद्धिः समाधौ न विधीयते ॥
त्रैगुण्यविषया वेदा निस्त्रैगुण्यो भवार्जुन ।
निर्द्वंद्वो नित्यसत्त्वस्थो निर्योगक्षेम आत्मवान् ॥
यावानर्थ उदपाने सर्वतः संप्लुतोदके ।
तावान्सर्वेषु वेदेषु ब्राह्मणस्य विजानतः ॥
यदा ते मोहकलिलं बुद्धिर्व्यतितरिष्यति ।
तदा गंतासि निर्वेदं श्रोतव्यस्य श्रुतस्य च ॥
श्रुतिविप्रतिपन्ना ते यदा स्थास्यति निश्चला ।
समाधावचला बुद्धिस्तदा योगमवाप्स्यसि ॥

(Ch. ii, 42-53.)

"The flowery speech of the foolish men who are always talking of 'Veda, Veda,' as if there were nothing else, filled with desires, greedy of paradise. ambitious of powers, craving after luxuries—they who allow their minds to be carried away by that deceptive speech, they never attain to the steadiness of the understanding which sees the Self in and by meditation. Rise above the (Karma-kanda, ritualism and literalism, of the) Vedas, Arjuna! Rise beyond the reach of the three *guna-s*, rise beyond the pairs of opposites, rise to the supremacy of the Self. To the man who knows the immensity of the Self, the whole of the Vedas is of no more use than is a small and shallow puddle in a time of widespread flood. When thy mind has crossed beyond its present confusion, then will it feel surfeited with all this endless repetition of hearsay (*shruta*, *shruti*, "that which is heard," tradition). Perplexed now by confusing *shrutis*, (of Karma-kanda, "ritual," and conventional ethics, based on hearsay, and not on ascertained essential Jnana-kanda, "scientific" and philosophical principles), when thy understanding succeeds in attaining steady contemplation of the Universal Self, then wilt thou attain yoga-union with that Self, realising It as thy-Self."

The teaching is further explained in the *Bhagavata*, by Krishna to Uddhava.

श्रौतेन जन्मनाऽथापि मुह्यंत्याम्नायवादिन: ।
कर्मण्यकोविदा: स्तब्धा. मूर्खा: पडिनमानिन: ॥
विप्रो राजन्यवैश्यौ च हरे: प्राप्ता: पदांतिकम् ।
वदंति चाटुकान्मूढा यया माध्व्या गिरोत्सुका: ॥
रजसा घोरसंकल्पा: कामुका अहिमन्यव: ।
दाभिका मानिन: पापा विहसंन्यच्युतप्रियान् ॥
फलश्रुतिं कुसुमिनां न वेदज्ञा वदंति हि ।
कामिन: कृपणा लुब्धा: पुष्पेषु फलबुद्धय: ॥
अग्निमुग्धा धूमतांता: स्वं लोकं न विदंति ते ।
न ते मामंग जानंति हृदिस्थं य इदं यत: ॥
उक्थशस्त्रा ह्यसुतृपो यथा नीहारचक्षुष: ।
ते मे मतमविज्ञाय परोक्षं विषयात्मका: ॥
हिंसाविहारा ह्यालब्धै: पशुभि: स्वसुखेच्छया ।
यजंते देवता यज्ञै: पितृभूतपतीन् खला: ॥

स्वप्नोपममम‍ुं लोकमसंतं श्रवणप्रियम् ।
आशिषो हृदि संकल्प्य त्यजंत्यर्थान् यथा वणिक् ।।
रजःसत्त्वतमोनिष्ठा रजःसत्त्वतमोजुषः ।
उपासत इन्द्रमुख्यान् देवादीन्न तथैव माम् ।।
इष्ट्वेह देवता यज्ञैर्गत्वा रंस्यामहे दिवि ।
तस्यांत इह भूयास्म महाशाला महाकुलाः ।।
एवं पुष्पितया वाचा व्याक्षिप्तमनसां नृणाम् ।
मानिनां जातिस्तब्धानां मद्वार्त्तापि न रोचते ।।
वेदा ब्रह्मात्मविषयास्त्रिकांडविषया इमे ।
परोक्षवादा ऋषयः परोक्षं च मम प्रियम् ।।
मां विधत्तेऽभिधत्ते मां विकल्प्यापोह्यते त्वहम् ।
एतावान्सर्ववेदार्थः शब्द आस्थाय मां भिदाम् ।
मायामात्रमनूद्यान्ते प्रतिषिध्य प्रसीदति ।। XI. v, xxi.

"Persons born in even good families, wherein the achievement of the second birth (regeneration) should be easy, are led astray by the honeyed words of (the outer) Scripture, immerse themselves in endless ritual, and imagine themselves to be very learned, when they are really only very foolish and very conceited . . . Lustful, implacable in their hates like serpents, dire in their separativeness, arrogant and vicious, they ridicule the lovers of the eternal all-pervading Self. Misty-eyed with avarice, blinded with the smoke of their blood-guilty sacrifices, sense-seeking, lustful and cruel, they know not Me, the Self who is this all, from whom is this all. They slay innocent animals in worship of low and false and foul spirits, to satisfy their own blood-thirstiness; and what ostensible gifts they make here are given in the spirit of the tradesman, with hope of much greater return in the shape of the dream-joys of other worlds and of a return to this in richer surroundings. To men deceived by such flowery words of the letter of the Scriptures, and puffed up with the pride of caste, all talk of the Eternal Self is utterly distasteful. They talk verbosely of Veda, but they know nothing of the hidden meaning of the Veda. The I, the Self, is ever hidden underneath forms. It is mysterious. The Rshis therefore speak of it in covers of mystery. Yet the whole Veda has no other purpose, in reality, than, through all sorts of disguises, to point the way to Me, the Supreme Self, to lead from *Karma* to *Jnana* of the Self."[67]

Buddha and Shankara also, and indeed all religious reformers, have battled against this deadly ritualism, which, like epidemics and plagues of weeds, insects, locusts, diseases, etc., periodically overwhelms and perverts human intelligence, so that that which was intended for the highest helping of humanity becomes its worst hinderer.

As the *Upanishat* says,

यद् देवा अकुर्वंस्तदसुरा अभिद्रुत्य पाप्मना अविध्यन् ।

"What the gods created to be virtuous, that the titans ran after and tainted with vice." Indeed the law is earlier. It governs the primal births themselves. Brahma, creating gods, created the titans also. God, creating angels, created Satan and the devils also. The Vedas, in their Karma-kanda too, lay down useful rules; but the excesses of human

---

[67] For a "curious coincidence" of thought, compare the following: "The Gnostics . . . asserted that it was impossible that a religion (the Jewish) which consisted of only bloody sacrifices and trifling ceremonies, and whose rewards as well as punishments were all of a carnal and temporal nature, could inspire the love of virtue, or restrain the impetuosity of passion." (GIBBON, *Roman Empire*, ch.xv.)

nature pervert them to mischief. Organisation of society becomes exclusive hereditary caste rigidity. Injunction to be pure leads to self-righteous contempt of others. Advice to be careful and clean in diet and in marriage, for individual and racial health, is misinterpreted into mere touch-me-not-ism. Truly the work of world-mending is unending! Maya deliberately creates myriad-faced error endlessly to serve as relieving background for the one eternal Truth.

## NOTE

For an example of excessive ritualism in the West, see Gibbon, *Roman Empire*, ch. 44. "Among savage nations the want of letters is imperfectly supplied by the use of visible signs, which awaken attention and perpetuate the remembrance of any public or private transactions. The jurisprudence of the first Romans exhibited the scenes of a pantomime; the words were adapted to the gestures, and the slightest error or neglect in the *forms* of proceeding was sufficient to annul the *substance* of the fairest claim . . . [Then follow many examples] . . . This occult science of the words and actions of law was the inheritance of the pontiffs and patricians." Even to-day, all "experts" of every art and craft and science tend to make a recondite mystery of their professional technicalities; H.G. Wells makes some trenchant observations on modern legal language and formalities in his *Outline of History*. The motive is natural and obvious, *viz.*, self-aggrandisement, in various ways.

The passage quoted above from Gibbon begins with a reference to savages. But the Romans of the period to which the paragraph refers were scarcely savages. For another example, from a highly civilised nation, see Michael MacDonagh's *The Pageant of Parliament*, which describes the ritual solemnly observed by the British Parliament even to-day, though it was instituted centuries ago, and must be causing smiles, now, even to those who observe it. It is a case of persistence of vestiges. In a country like India the persistence is directly helped by the "vested interests" of a whole large and intelligent section of the people to whom it has unfortunately become a means of living, and who are therefore interested in the rest of the people remaining un-intelligent and un-inquisitive.

But we also find that Krishna himself, while condemning dead formalism, hints, in the quotation from the *Bhagavata* above, that there is a deeper meaning underneath the outer word of the Veda. The rather obscure *Gita*-verse, also, which compares the Vedas to a shallow puddle, *may* be interpreted in another way. The word *uda-pana*, ordinarily meaning a *small pool* of drinking water, may, with the context, be construed as comparing the Vedas to "a *great reservoir* heaving with deep waters in time of flood". A paraphrase, in the *Sanatsujata Gita*, of this verse, is also double-sensed. The expression there is उदपाने महति, which *may* be read as उदपानेऽमहति. Manu also speaks of the *rahasya*, the "secret," of the Veda, its *jnana-kanda* of *knowledge*, as distinguished from the *karma-kanda* of *ritual* (ii. 140, 165). And H. P. Blavatsky, in *The Secret Doctrine*, refers to the Vedas as being the work of "Initiates", embodying "Occult Science," and yielding many interpretations with the help of "seven keys".

We also find that similar beliefs have gathered round other Scriptures, of historically recent origin, like the Bible and the Quran. Thus Lindsay, in his *History of the Reformation*, Vol.I, says: "The Mediaeval Church forbade to laymen, over and over again, the reading of the Vulgate" (the Latin translaion of the Bible, made by Jerome, *circa* A. D. 400; the Vedas, it is well known, were forbidden by their custodians to the "lowest caste"; the Church and the State, when perverse and selfish, everywhere deliberately spread ignorance and superstition instead of, as is their duty to do, knowledge and enlightenment). "Then arose the four senses of the Scripture, literal, moral, allegorical, and anagogic, which enable the reader to draw any meaning he pleases from any portion of Scripture". The Vedas are also said to be *kama-dhenu*, "the cow of plenty": one can get from them what one likes; the *Nirukta* mentions the different ways in which they may be interpreted, *aitihasika*, *yaugika*, *yajnika*, *adhyatmika*, etx. "Pope Innocent III reprobated the translation of the Scriptures into the vernaculars, because ordinary laymen, and especially women, have not sufficient intelligence to understand them." It is well known that the Vedas are claimed to be "the word of Brahma," *Brahma-vakya*, or, if possible, even older than Brahma. So the Bible is claimed to be Gospel, *i.e.*, God-spell, God-spoken. So the Quran is regarded by its followers as *Kalam-ullah*, "the word of God". "The substance of the Quran," says Gibbon (in ch. 50 of his *Roman Empire*), "according to (Muhammad) himself or his disciples is uncreated and eternal, subsisting in the essence of the Deity, and inscribed with a pen of light on the table of his everlasting decrees."

Apart from possible or impossible secret meanings, the reconciliation of such rival and conflicting claims is that *all truth* is eternal, and the work, not of man, but of Deity. The truths of mathematics, the real laws and fact of every science, are obviously not the inventions but only the discoveries, of human beings. are not their work but the work of Nature and her God, the Eternal Self. The Veda, which means all true "knowledge," may well be *a-paurusheya,* "non-human," in this sense. Unhappily, the *exalte* mood of the over-faithful, the blind devotees, or the astuteness of the schemers, gives a personal turn to the impersonal, changes universal religion into sectarianism, and causes troubles and tragedies—which too have their place in the World-process! What Gibbon says of Islam (ch. 50 of his work), applies to all "faiths," more or less; they are "compounded of an eternal truth and a necessary fiction—That there is only one God, and that (so-and-so) is the (only) apostle of God." Yet the fiction is converted easily into fact by replacing the words "the only apostle" with the words "one of the perpetual series of apostles": and may, therefore, at first sight, seem not "necessary"; but, yet. again. metaphysic seems to say that the seed of truth needs the manure of falsehood to sprout and flourish.

There are probably hundreds of sects. *pantha-s,* living their life, to-day, in East and West ; each has its *guru,* its spiritual head; probably each of these heads claims extraordinary, mystical, superphysical powers, but declines to give proofs thereof. yet receives faith from some. "As often as he (the prophet) is pressed by . . demands," ays Gibbon *(ibid.).* "he involves himself in the obscure (talk) of vision and prophecy, appeals to the internal proofs of his doctrine, and shields himself behind the providence of God, who refuses those signs and wonders that would depreciate the merit of faith and aggravate the guilt of infidelity." Yet common sense demands that where proof is refused on the one side, belief should be refused on the other. If the one is forbidden, so is the other. Of course, such "internal proofs" as are available should be carefully judged with open mind. The chapters of Gibbon's *Roman Empire,* which deal with the birth and the early years of Christianity and Islam will be found very instructive by the student of religious origins.

As to why a work like the Vedas, if it really does contain deep science. should be worded so as to more easily yield ill meaning than good—this is a very difficult question. I have tried to deal with it in the preface to the *Pranava-Vada.* We can only say, Good and Evil are inseparable, as shine and shade. Gods and titans are step-brothers. *Demon est Deus inversus.* Truth and Error are imitations, copies, looking-glass reflections and images of each other, but reversed, opposed. *Vidya* and *A-vidya* are twin sisters, nay, forms of one and the same Maya-Shakti. As the *Bhagavata* says,

सत्यं पुष्पफलं विद्याद् अनृतं मूलमात्मनः ॥

"Truth, Wisdom, is the flower-and-fruit; Falsehood, Error, is the root—of this Tree of the Self's Life, the World-process." This is to be regarded as an explanation, perhaps also a consolation, but scarcely as counsel to acquiescent action.

On the whole, seeing that this is the age of reason and of science, of the development of intellect, of the "fifth principle" in Theosophical phrase, it is much to be wished, and effort should be made, that there may be less of mystery-mongering and sensationalism in the otherwise very desirable and very laudable endeavor to revive spirituality (—"revivalist" has become a byword in the West—), and more of spiritual rationalism and the spirit of scientific demonstration, under proper conditions, of course. Krishna demonstrated his powers (though the demonstrations have been subsequently grossly exaggerated, and his human "weaknesses" have been idealised away), and taught spiritual rationalism, and has therefore rightly deserved a reasonable amount of faith and devotion.

## The Gita and the Anu-Gita

Beyond and above all Krishna's other great works, stands his work as the teacher of the *Gita*, wherein he concentrated, with the electrical focussing of war conditions, the quintessence of the deepest, the most ancient, and the most practical and real ethics and philosophy, into a few hundred verses, for the enlightenment of the sorely perplexed understanding of Arjuna, and of hundreds of subsequent generations. The *Maha-bharata* incorporates another utterance of Krishna—also in the shape of teaching given to his dearest friend Arjuna—and known as the *Anu-gita*. But this work is not much studied, although it seems to be almost indispensable for the right understading of the *Gita*. It is expressly a reutterance of and a supplement to the earlier work and embodies much more systematic philosophy.

The circumstances in which this luminous discourse was given may be mentioned. After the great war, Krishna dwelt with the Pandavas, helping them to reorganise the disturbed *rashtra*, the state, and set it all in order. Then, one day, wandering about in the halls and gardens of Indraprastha, he said to his beloved friend Arjuna: "Many days have I dwelt here, dear friend, because I take joy in seeing thee. But Bala-rama and my many kinsfolk and large household at Dwara-wati wish to see me, and I must go to them now." And Arjuna was depressed, and said: "Yes, I see you must go. But before you go, tell me again what you told me on the battle-field for the enlightenment of my bewildered mind. I seem to have lost it all amidst the subsequent distractions. But my mind craves after those deep inner things again and again."

तत्सर्वं पुरुषव्याघ्र नष्टं मे व्यग्रचेतसः ।
मम कौतूहलं त्वस्ति तेष्वर्थेषु पुनः पुनः ।
भवांस्तु द्वारकां गन्ता न चिरादिव माधव ॥

*Anu-gita, Ch. i.*

Then Krishna : "Now I like it very ill that thou hast dull-wittedly let go the eternal secret and sacred wisdom that I gave to thee then. I was in a high mood of *yoga* at that time and the memory will not come back to me. Thou art surely lacking in faith and very lacking in intelligence. It is not possible for me to repeat it all over again exactly. But I will tell thee, instead, an historical dialogue which will equally enlighten thy mind and help thee to attain the goal." All which scolding of poor Arjuna does not seem very reasonable, though very human, and very characteristic of benevolent teachers. When Krishna himself had forgotten what he had said and found it impossible to repeat it, it was hard on Arjuna to be reprimanded for doing the same thing! But great men may do what smaller men may not! And Krishna went on to deliver the *Anu-Gita*, which is more systematic than the other, and very illuminating, though regrettably neglected. And fortunately for humanity, though the memories of both Krishna and Arjuna were so unreliable, Vyasa has somehow mysteriously managed to preserve both the first and the second *Gita-s*. When Narada advised Vyasa to sing the glories of Krishna, he counselled him also to see and hear the past, with all its secrets, everlastingly recorded in the Universal Supra-Consciousness, by means of the inner senses he had won by his yoga-discipline; and Vyasa did so. But Krishna, at the time he was asked by Arjuna, was perhaps in a lazy mood, and thinking of his large "household," and disinclined for special yoga-effort. So he confined himself to the exercise of his ordinary mind, which was extra-ordinary enough!

Incidentally, in the authorship of these *Gita-s*, we have an outstanding confirmation of the fact that no one can be an efficient professor of a subject unless he is in living touch with that department of the real daily communal or national life which he professes to study and teach; that philosophy, in order to be realised, in order to become real, must be not only thought out in closet or cave or other solitude, but must be drawn forth thence and applied to, and tested on the battle-fields of life. And it is very characteristic of the Indian mind and culture and civilisation that the veteran generalissimo of a vast army, like Arjuna, should want to run away from the battle, at the last moment, because of ethical scruples, and should be fortified for fighting by a metaphysical discourse, given then and there, on the Eternal Principles of the Universe.

The whole and sole teaching of the *Gita* is very pragmatic, very practical, and very rational. That teaching is, in brief: "Do your duty, not out of blind faith in any petty, paltry, ritualistic and dictatorial conventions, but after ascertaining it in the light of Atma-vidya—the all-co-ordinating, all-illuminating science; and then do it without craving for fruit, fearless of consequences, sure that right resolve and right effort can never go in vain, but will always bring right result, soon or late."

### The High Spiritual Rationalism of the Gita

The *Gita* is indeed a very manual of Rationalism. But it is not the rationalism which bases upon and starts from the *data* of the senses. These *data* are obviously very limited, variable, perishing, uncertain. Reasoning founded upon them, therefore, necessarily remains incomplete, imperfect, lop-sided, tinged with the bias of personal experience and feeling, individualist, separatist, extremist, ever-shifting; it sees only one side of any question at one time, and, therefore inherently and inevitably gives rise to irreconcilable and endless controversy.[68] Instead, the rationalism of the *Gita*, its *buddhi-vada*, takes its stand upon, and proceeds from, and is ever returning to and circling round, the One and only absolutely certain and Immutable Fact, *viz.*, the Self. It is therefore unvarying (more so, if possible, than mathematics), all-co-ordinating, perfect. It leads to reconciliation of opposite opinions, to synthesis of all aspects of every

[68] तर्कोऽप्रतिष्ठः ।

problem, and hence to finality.[69] It takes comprehensive views, outlooks as well as inlooks, of both the sides of every question, and so provides balanced and correct answers to them all. It is Spiritual Rationalism as contra-distinguished from Material Rationalism. The two, *sattvika buddhi* and *tamasa buddhi* (*Gita*, xviii, 30-32), are as an object and its image reflected in water; very similar, yet very opposite; the right side has become the left, the left the right; the top has become the bottom, the bottom the top. Falsehood is indeed the inverted copy of Truth. *Demon est Deus inversus*. This difference of basic philosophy has far-reaching consequences in all departments of life, in the aims, principles, methods, practices, of pedagogics, domestics, economics, civics, politics, laws, arts, sciences, religion. In the domains of all these, the Spiritual Civilisation, inspired by Spiritual Rationalism, the civilisation of *Daivi Sampat* ("godly" qualities), predominant love, sympathy, alliance, co-operation, unselfish philanthropy, the civilisation of the *higher* Socialism of moral culture and self-guiding inner impulsion. will show differences from the Material Civilisation, inspired by Material Rationalism, of *Asuri Sampat* ("titanic" or "demoniac" powers and possessions), perdominant strife, arrogance, lust, hate, greed, selfish struggle, unchecked competition and the lower Individualism or, what in effect is the same thing, the dictatorial *lower* Socialism of artificial and forced devices and the penal code and mechanical outer compulsion (*Gita*, xvi). As is the outlook upon and inlook into life, as is the idea of what are the fundamental and supreme values and ends of life, the greatest good-s,

---

69 वेदस्य अन्तः, वेदान्तः ।

the *purush-artha-s*, as is the philosophy of life, whether that philosophy be conscious or unconscious, so will be the life.

It has been said above that the Self is the only indubitable and ever unchanging Fact. See. The senses prove the existence of sensable objects. But what proves the existence of these senses themselves? Has any ear ever heard itself; has any skin touched, eye seen, nose smelt, or tongue tasted itself ? No. *I* hear, touch, see, taste, smell. And *I* am *aware* of doing so, through, with, by means of, an ear, a skin, etc. *I* have made my self. *I* have *become*, an ear, a skin, ete., with the wish, for the purpose, to hear sounds, touch tacts, see sights, taste savors, smell odors.[70] *My conciousness* proves to me the existence of these senses as well as of their objects. at the same time that it proves its own existence to me, *i.e.*, proves my own existence to myself. "The diapason closing full in Man," "Man is the centre of the Universe," Man is the crown of creation"—all these are ludicrously false conceits, if "man" means the human body of flesh and blood and bone. But if "man" indicates the Self, then these statements are uttermost truths. The doctrine propounded by some philosophers of the West, that conceivability is the test of truth, is justifiable similarly, if we interpret the phrase as meaning that Consciousness is the ultimate proof of all proofs, and of all provable things, as well as of itself. The sun lights itself as well as all else.

To whom do the senses belong? To the Me, to the I. To whom, and for whom, do they prove the worlds that they do prove? To the I, for the Me. *Cogito, ergo sum*, "I think, therefore I am," is erroneous superfluity of words. It would be more correct to say: " I am, therefore I think."

---

70 शृणवानीति श्रोत्रमभवत् ।, etc., *Chhandogya-Upanishat*, viii.12. 4.

*Sum* is enough. "I am." The one fact, and the only fact, which is absolutely beyond question, which can be disputed by none, which is utterly self-evident, is that "I am". Mountains, oceans, this solid seeming globe of the earth, sun, moon, stars, have come into existence, are going out of it, will pass away, over and over again; all these vast things, as well as the most minute, *may be* dreams, *are* dreams; but the Dreamer is not a dream; He, I, never passes in and out; I am; I always am; even in dreams, in wildest illusions, and nothing can be wilder than what I am seeing with my physical eyes, even in slumber, "I am". Hence the ancient Scriptures rightly say: "My first name is 'Ahmi' (I am; Skt. *Asmi*, I am, *Aham*, I)"; (*Ormazd Yasht*, 7.) "I am that I am; . . . I am hath sent me unto you"; (*Exodus*, iii, 14.) "I am (*i.e.*, the I is) God and there is none-else"; (*Isaiah*, xlv, 5, 6, 18, 22; xlvi, 9). "Inni An-Allahu la ilaha illa Ana; I, verily the I, is God; none-other-than-I is God";(*Quran*, Surat-ut-Ta-Ha, xxv, 14.) "Naught-else-than-I is";(*Chhandogya*, vii, 7, 24; *Brhadaranyaka*, i, 4, 1,; *Gita*, vii, 7; and *Bhagavata*, II, xiii, 24.) "I is Atma"; (*Gita*, x, 20.)

But the True, Essential, Infinite, Universal, "I" (which may as well be called the all-including "We") must be very carefully distinguished from the pseudo-infinite, false, individual, singular, separate I's which are produced by the reflection of the Universal I in the pseudo-infinite particular forms of matter. Again, *Demon est Deus inversus;* egoism is the Ego inverted and perverted; the all-pervasive, all-inclusive, Universal Self is the opposite of the separative, exclusive, selfish, individual selves. Yet all these latter are the reflections of the One Universal Self. The Essence underneath each one of these reflections is the Same. It is of this "We", of this "Common" I, this Common Principle of Consciousness running through all "proper" I's, that the *Gita* declares over and over again,

ज्ञानं तेऽहं सविज्ञानमिदं वक्ष्याम्यशेषतः ।
यज्ज्ञात्वा नेह भूयोऽन्यज्ज्ञातव्यमवशिष्यते ।।
अहं कृत्स्नस्य जगतः प्रभवः प्रलयस्तथा ।।
" मत्तः परतरं नान्यत्किंचिद् " अस्ति धनंजय ।
मयि सर्वमिदं प्रोतं सूत्रे मणिगणा इव ।। (vii, 2, 6, 7.)
इदं तु ते गुह्यतमं प्रवक्ष्याम्यनसूयवे ।
ज्ञानं विज्ञानसहितं यज्ज्ञात्वा मोक्ष्यसेऽशुभात् ।।
मया ततमिदं सर्वं जगदव्यक्तमूर्तिना ।
मत्स्थानि सर्वभूतानि न चाहं तेष्ववस्थितः ।
न च मत्स्थानि भूतानि पश्य मे योगमैश्वरम् ।।
अवजानन्ति मां मूढा मानुषीं तनुमाश्रितम् ।
परं भावमजानन्तो मम भूतमहेश्वरम् ।।
पिताऽहमस्य जगतो माता धाता पितामहः ।
गतिर्भर्ता प्रभुः साक्षी निवासः शरणं सुहृत् ।।

(ix, 1, 4, 5, 11, 17, 18.)

अहमात्मा गुडाकेश सर्वभूताशयस्थितः ।
अहमादिश्च मध्यं च भूतानामन्त एव च ।। (x, 20.)
क्षरः सर्वाणि भूतानि कूटस्थोऽक्षर उच्यते ।
उत्तमः पुरुषस्त्वन्यः परमात्मेत्युदाहृतः ।।
यस्मात्क्षरमतीतोऽहमक्षरादपि चोत्तमः ।
अतोऽस्मि लोके वेदे च प्रथितः पुरुषोत्तमः ।।
इति गुह्यतमं शास्त्रं इदमुक्तं मयाऽनघ ।
एतद्बुध्वा बुद्धिमान् स्यात् कृतकृत्यश्च भारत ।। (xv, 16-20.)

इति ते ज्ञानमाख्यातं गुह्याद्गुह्यतरं मया ।
विमृश्यैतदशेषेण यथेच्छसि तथा कुरु ।।
सर्वगुह्यतमं भूयः शृणु मे परमं वचः ।
मन्मना भव मद्भक्तो मद्याजी मां नमस्कुरु ।।
सर्वधर्मान्परित्यज्य मामेकं शरण व्रज ।
अहं त्वां सर्वपापेभ्यो मोक्षयिष्यामि मा शुचः ।।
य इदं परमं गुह्यं मद्भक्तेष्वभिधास्यति ।
भक्ति मयि परां कृत्वा मामेवैष्यत्यसंशयम् ।।

(ix, 34; and xviii, 63-68.)

In the above quotation, all those verses of the *Gita* are gathered in which it is said that "This is the whole of knowledge, after knowing which nothing remains to be known; this is the deepest secret of all; more secret than all other secrets." What is this essence of knowledge, this uttermost truth, this most profound secret, and yet also the most familiar, the nearest, the dearest? It is this, says Krishna, and says every soul, every I, in its deepest heart, also:

"The I is the womb and the tomb of the whole world, its birth-place as well as its sepulchre. *Naught-else-than-I* is. All the *This*, the *Else*, all facts, all acts, all experiences, all objects, are threaded on the I, as gems on silk (for, quite obviously, the I, an I, some I, wears, bears, does, all, any, every, form and name and act; "I" am so-and-so, "I" do this-and-this). The I as the Unmanifest, the Unconscious, the Supra-Conscious Cause, has spread forth all the This as Manifest Effect. All things are in the I, not the I in the things; nor indeed are the things in the I, (for the I is naught-else-than-I, and "things," "Else" "This," is naught, is Not); such is the marvel of the I, the wonder of the sovereign yoga, the unique conjunction, of the I with the This. The ignorant, error-blinded, slight the I masked in human frame, un-wotting of Its transcendant, eternal, infinite supremacy over all things finite. The I is the father, the mother, the nurse, the tacher, the sweet-hearted friend, the spouse, the owner, the master, the witness, the supervisor, the spectator, the goal, the refuge, the abiding resting-place, of all the This, of all the beings and contents of the World-process. Perishing, fleeting, changing are all finite things and beings that compose the ever-flowing stream of the This; unperishing, fixed, changeless, is the rock-seated Witness, the I. Because the Infinite and Universal I transcends the ever-perishing This, because it is higher and fuller than the unperishing *abstract* I also, therefore is the *Supreme* I known in the outer world as well as the inner world of sacred scriptural wisdom as the Purushottama, the Highest and Best Self. No *Other*-dharma-s help. Give up all *Other*-dharma-s, dharma-s which lean on any *other*-than-the-I for support. Take refuge in *Swa*-dharma, *Self*-dharma, in the I alone (all-one). Direct thy whole mind, heart, devotion, sacrifice, obeisance, unto the Universal I alone. The I realised as all-pervading, and therefore as the very Principle of Love and Service and Duty and Virtue, will free thee from all sins and miseries. Doubt not, fear not, sorrow no more".[71]

---

[71]See *The Science of Peace*, or the last three chapers of the present writer's Hindi book, समन्वय (*Samanvaya*. recently published by the Bharati-Bhandar, Benares), for a fuller exposition of the significance of "Naught-Else-than-I is," and of the distinction and difference between (1) the Purush-ottama. Paramatma; (2) the Akshara. Kutastha, Pratyag-atma,

As the verses show, all possible relations, parent, etc., expressible by any prepositions, are exhausted as between the I and the This, the Subject and the Object. The whole world of all possible objects (physical or superphysical, familiar or unfamiliar, commonplace or mystical and gran-

---

Avyakta Purusha; (3) the Jiv-atma, Vyakta Purusha, and (4) the Kshara, ever-changing, Many, Mula-prakrti. The English equivalents would be (1) the Universal Self, (2) the Abstract Self, (3) the Individual Self, and (4) Root-Matter or Root-Nature (the Nature of the Self). In Sufism, the corresponding words seem to be (1) Ahd, (2) Wahd, (3) Wahid or Fard, and (4) Shay (thing) or Maad-dah (Root-Matter) or Adam (Non-being). (1) Ahdiyat, (2) Wahdat, (3) Wahidiyat, (4) Kasrat would respectively be (1) Universality or Absoluteness, (2) Unity, Oneness, (3) Individuality, singularity, particularity, and (4) Manyness: in Samskrt, (1) Sarvika-ta, (2) Eka-ta, (3) Vyakti-ta, (4) Aneka-ta, or Nana-tva. In terms of Samskrt and English grammar, Param-atma or Purush-ottama may be regarded as the *uttama purusha*, the first person plural (or collective all-including singular); Pratyag-atma as the same but in the aspect of abstract singular; Jiv-atma as the *madhyama pursha* (the "middle" person, between, and combining, Spirit and Matter; Man, in whom God and Nature meet and manifest), the second person; Mula-prakrti as the *prathama purusha*, the third person. These may be said to correspond broadly to the three persons of the Trinity also, Mula-prakrti being there replaced by its first manifest appearance as Buddhi, named in various ways and aspects as the Holy Ghost, the sixth principle, etc. It seems that the Sufis also use the expressions (1) Ayn-i-murakkab or Khuda-i-murakkab, (2) Ayn-i-mujarrad or Khuda-i-mujarrad, (3) Ayn-i-muayyan or Khuda-i-muayyan for (1) Paramatma, (2) Pratyagatma, and (3) Jivatma, respectively. *Kasrat-dar-Wahdat* and *Wahdat-dar-Kasrat*, Many-in-One and One-in-Many, expresses the idea of the *Gita*-verse,

यदा भूतपृथग्भावमेकस्थमनुपश्यति ।
तत एव च विस्तारं ब्रह्म संपद्यते तदा ॥ xiii, 30.

"When man sees the separate Manyness of things rooted in the One, and the One branching out into the Many, then his knowledge becomes complete, then he becomes Brahman."

diose, clear and distinct or vague and hazy and cloudy, small, trivial, prosaic, sordid, or great, sentimental, exalted, poetical, practical or ideal) is *in* the I, the Self, the subject; is *of* the I, is the Self's property; is *from*, comes forth *out of*, the I, derives whatever appearance of substance it has, from the substance, the Conscious positivity, of the I; is *for* the I, dances its vast dance and plays its endless play, and infinitely displays itself in countless forms and incessant drama, for the sake of the I, is experienced, enjoyed and ensorrowed, by the I, none-else; is *by* the I, is created by the ideation, the wil-ful imagination, of the I, is generated, evolved, maintained, ruled, inspired, vivified, whirled about, by the waking up of the I, and is also destroyed and dissolved, in the same way, by the withdrawal of the attention, the going to sleep, of the I; is *to* the I, returns to the I constantly, retires into and disappears in it perpetually at sleep, even as it proceeds from the same I continually at waking; and, finally, the whole world-process *is* the I itself, is identical with it, as the dream is with the dreamer; but, also, at the same time, the I transcends the This, is beyond all the This, denies and negates the This, repudiates all relationship with the This, which repudiation itself constitutes the indissoluble relationship between the two. All the above-mentioned prepositional relations between the I and the This may be summed up in the following,

यस्मिन् यस्य च यस्माच्च यस्मै येन च य तथा।
यश्चेदं च परश्चास्मात् तस्मै सर्वात्मने नमः ॥

The same truth of the manifold relationship between Purusha and Prakrti, Spirit and Matter, is indicated in another *Gita*-verse,

अहं क्रतुरहं यज्ञ: स्वधाऽहमहमौषधम् ।
मन्त्रोऽहमहमेवाज्यमहमग्निरहं हुतम् ॥ (ix, 16.)

"The I is the Will-to-do, the I is the whole deed of sacrifice (or "creative art"–the Samskrt word *kratu* may mean both, and both here signify the whole World-process, which is the Self's artistic creation and sacri-fice, *i.e.*, "good act," by means of Self-sacrifice, Self-abnegation and Not-Self-[=This] assertion), the I is the progenitive motive of self-expression and self-perpetuation, the I is the life-maintaining herb (food in general), the I is the ideation and the magic rune (which embodies and carries into effect that ideation, Sound or the Word being the first sensuous manifestation), the I is the vitality-storing liquid poured into the Fire, the I is the Fire (which transforms the seed thrown into it), and the I is every single act of offering and every single substance offered up, also."

All the different systems of philosophy, of faith, of worship, which have ever arisen, differ from one another only in this that they emphasise, one by one, turn by turn, in the growth of humanity (and they do this also by the inner urge and command of that same inseated, inspiring, un-conscious, supra-conscious I), one or another of these *a-sankhya*-(countless) relations (*yoga-s*) of the *sankhya*-Purusha (the Purusha of the Sankhya philosophy, the *samyak-khyata*, the well-known, the self-evident I, the unconcealed God) and the *sankhya*-Prakrti (the equally obvious Nature of God, the pseudo-infinite contents of the Self, the countless vestures of Matter which the Spirit is ever putting on and off).[72]

---

[72]The main views, under which all the others may be grouped, are: (1) Arambha-vada, (2) Parinamavada, (3) Adhyasa-(or vivarta, abhasa, maya, advaita, etc.) -vada. Broad correspondences are: (1) Dvaita, (2)

And all these will be found summed up in that "uttermost, deepest, final, secret" which Krishna refers to four times.[73] in the course of the *Gita* (*vide* the verses quoted above): "Negating all *others*, all *This's*, hold fast the I. The Full and perfect I is the Purush-ottama which includes both the abstract Purusha and the concrete Prakrti. The wise abide in the I-not-others. There is Naught-Else-than-I." The word "not-other" (*an-anya*) occurs eight times[73] in the *Gita*, mostly in the course of the veiled disclosures of this "secret of all secrets," contained in the three simple words, "I—other (=this)-not."[74]

This Atma is the self-evident locus and focus, the impregnable, unshakable, unquestionable basis, and also the inexhaustible and unquenchable fountain, of all Buddhi, all experienec (of all kinds, planes, worlds, better known or lesser known) and all reasoning founded thereon, all the highest and deepest rationalism, which is able to see all sides of every question and is able to harmonise and synthesise them all, to reconcile all contradictions-because all differences, all contradictions, and all other possible relationships and aspects are within the Self. This Buddhi, in the larger universal sense

---

Vishisht-advaita, (3) Shuddh-advaita; (1) Bhakti-marga, (2) Karma-marga, (3) Jnanamarga; in western philosophy, (1) the theory of popular causation, (2) of scientific causation, (3) (of metaphysical causation, not yet distinctly recognised as such), or (1) Creation. (2) Transformation, (3) Ideation, Will-and-Imagination; in terms of theology, (1) Theism, (2) Pantheism, (3) Monism; in Sufi phrase, (1) Ijadiyah (*hama az ust*), (2) Shuhudiyah (and Dahriya, *hama andar ust*), (3) Wujudiya (*hama-ust*). See *The Science of Peace.*

[73] See Word-Index in Annie Besant and Bhagavan Das's *Bhagavad-Gita.*

[74] See *The Science of Peace.*

of Mahat, is Cosmic Intelligence, or, rather, *is* the whole, and, in the more limited individual sense, *cognises* (when its *sattva* element is not overpowered by its *rajas* or *tamas*) the outlines and main principles, of the Scheme of the manifold relationships between the I and the This, the Network, the Web, the *Sutra*, of the Laws and Facts of Nature, the Self's Nature, Purusha's Prakrti, the Laws and Facts which flow forth from, or, indeed, constitute, the Nature of the Self, the Nature which is the whole World-Process: and such *sattvika buddhi* is a force for harmony and reconciliation; it makes for unity in diversity.

After, or, indeed, simultaneously and side by side with, the Atma (Param-Atma, Para-Brahm, Param-Eshwara, Maha-Deva, Allahu-Akbar, all of which mean literally the same thing, *viz.*, "Greatest God" "beside-whom-there-is-no-other, A-dwitiya, Wahdahu-la-sharik-ilah,"[75] "One-not-a-second")[76], that which is most important is this Buddhi, which is to the Atma as light is to the Sun. The two are inseparable, scarcely even distinguishable.

In accordance with this fact we find that the word of greatest frequency of occurrence in the *Gita* is "Atma," with its declensional forms and their equivalents. "Aham," "Mam," "Mama," "Me," "Mat," etc.; and that the next degree of frequency belongs to "Buddhi," and its synonyms and allies "Jnana," "Prajna," "Dhih," etc., and their various terminational forms and compounds with other words.[77]

---

[75] Sufis.

[76] Bible, *Ecclesiastes*, ch. 4.

[77] See the Word-Index to the *Gita*.

Some of the most significant verses of the *Gita* regarding Buddhi may be gathered here.

एषा तेऽभिहिता सांख्ये बुद्धिर्योगे त्विमां शृणु ।
बुद्ध्या युक्तो यया पार्थ कर्मबन्धं प्रहास्यसि ।।
बुद्धौ शरणमन्विच्छ . . . बुद्धिनाशात्प्रणश्यति ।।
व्यवसायात्मिका बुद्धिरेकेह कुरुनन्दन ।
बुद्धियुक्तो जहातीह उभे सुकृतदुष्कृते ।।
कर्मजं बुद्धियुक्ता हि फलं त्यक्त्वा मनीषिणः ।
जन्मबन्धविनिर्मुक्ताः पदं गच्छन्त्यनामयम् ।।
प्रसन्नचेतसो ह्याशु बुद्धिः पर्यवतिष्ठते ।।
नास्ति बुद्धिरयुक्तस्य न चायुक्तस्य भावना ।
न चाभावयतः शान्तिरशान्तस्य कुतः सुखम् ।।
यदा ते मोहकलिलं बुद्धिर्व्यतितरिष्यति ।
तदा गन्तासि निर्वेदं श्रोतव्यस्य श्रुतस्य च ।।
श्रुतिविप्रतिपन्ना ते यदा स्थास्यति निश्चला ।
समाधावचला बुद्धिस्तदा योगमवाप्स्यसि ।।
प्रजहाति यदा कामान्सर्वान्पार्थ मनोगतान् ।
आत्मन्येवात्मना तुष्टः स्थितप्रज्ञस्तदोच्यते ।।
दुःखेष्वनुद्विग्नमनाः सुखेषु विगतस्पृहः ।
वीतरागभयक्रोधः स्थितधीर्मुनिरुच्यते ।। (ii, 39-66.)
यः सर्वत्रानभिस्नेहः तत्तत्प्राप्य शुभाशुभम् ।
नाभिनन्दति न द्वेष्टि तस्य प्रज्ञा प्रतिष्ठिता ।।
इन्द्रियाणि पराण्याहुरिन्द्रियेभ्यः परं मनः ।
मनसस्तु परा बुद्धिर्यो बुद्धेः परतस्तु सः ।।
एवं बुद्धेः परं बुद्धा संस्तभ्यात्मानमात्मना ।
जहि शत्रुं महाबाहो कामरूपं दुरासदम् ।। (iii, 42-43.)
कर्मण्यकर्म यः पश्येदकर्मणि च कर्म यः ।
स बुद्धिमान्मनुष्येषु स युक्तः कृत्स्नकर्मकृत् ।।

यस्य सर्वे समारम्भाः कामसंकल्पवर्जिताः ।
ज्ञानाग्निदग्धकर्माणं तमाहुः पण्डितं बुधा : ।।
श्रेयान्द्रव्यमयाद्यज्ञाज्ज्ञानयज्ञः परंतप ।
सर्वं कर्माखिलं पार्थ ज्ञाने परिसमाप्यते ।।
उपदेक्ष्यन्ति ते ज्ञानं ज्ञानिनस्तत्त्वदर्शिनः ।
यज्ज्ञात्वा न पुनर्मोहमेवं यास्यसि पाण्डव ।।
येन भूतान्यशेषेण द्रक्ष्यस्यात्मन्यथो मयि ।
सर्वं ज्ञानप्लवेनैव वृजिनं संतरिष्यसि ।।
ज्ञानाग्निः सर्वकर्माणि भस्मसात्कुरुतेऽर्जुन ।
न हि ज्ञानेन सदृशं पवित्रमिह विद्यते ।।
ज्ञानं लब्ध्वा परां शान्तिमचिरेणाधिगच्छति । (iv, 18-39.)
सुखमात्यन्तिकं यत्तद्बुद्धिग्राह्यमतीन्द्रियम् ।।
बुद्ध्या विशुद्धया युक्तो धृत्यात्मानं नियम्य च ।
विमुच्य निर्ममः शान्तो ब्रह्मभूयाय कल्पते ।।
(vi, 21; xvii. 51, 53.)

चतुर्विधा भजंते मां जनाः सुकृतिनोऽर्जुन ।
आर्त्तो जिज्ञासुरर्थार्थी ज्ञानी च भरतर्षभ ।।
तेषां ज्ञानी नित्ययुक्त एकभक्तिर्विशिष्यते ।
प्रियो हि ज्ञानिनोऽत्यर्थमहं स च मम प्रियः ।।
उदाराः सर्व एवैते ज्ञानी त्वात्मैव मे मतः ।
आस्थितः स हि युक्तात्मा मामेवानुत्तमां गतिम् ।।
(vii, 16-18.)

बुद्धिर्बुद्धिमतामस्मि ...... ज्ञानं ज्ञानवतामहम् ।।
(vii, 10; x, 38.)

तेषां सततयुक्तानां भजतां प्रीतिपूर्वकम् । (x, 10.)
ददामि बुद्धियोगं तं येन मामुपयान्ति ते ।। (xv, 20.)
इति गुह्यतमं शास्त्रमिदमुक्तं मयाऽनघ ।
एतद्बुध्वा बुद्धिमान् स्यात् कृतकृत्यश्च भारत ।।

सर्वभूतेषु येनैकं भावमव्ययमीक्षते ।
अविभक्तं विभक्तेषु तज्ज्ञानं विद्धि सात्त्विकम् ॥
प्रवृत्ति च निवृत्ति च कार्याऽकार्ये भयाऽभये ।
बन्धं मोक्षं च या वेत्ति बुद्धिः सा पार्थ सात्त्विकी ॥
चेतसा सर्वकर्माणि मयि सन्यस्य मत्परः ।
बुद्धियोगमुपाश्रित्य मच्चित्तः सततं भव ॥

(xviii, 20 30, 37, 57.)

यत् तदग्रे विषमिव परिणामेऽमृतोपमम् ।
तत्सुखं सात्त्विकं प्रोक्त आत्मबुद्धिप्रसादजम् ॥

"The Understanding (Buddhi) of Life, the outlook and inlook upon Life everywhere, given by the Sankhya and the Yoga philosophies, is the same in essence and practical bearing. Endowed with that Understanding, that rational intelligence, acting in accord with its dictates, man is able to avoid the fetters that are otherwise created by all action, which is ordinarily motived by the emotions and passions which bind souls to one another, and not motived by the sense of duty, the discharging of what is due, which unlooses those bonds. Seek refuge, then, in Right Understanding, Reason, Intelligence. He who loses Reason loses himself (in the ordinary sense, as well as in the special Theosophical sense, which is only a sublimation and expansion of the ordinary sense, *viz*., that loss of connection with the sixth principle involves dissolution of the fifth also, practically and comparatively; though metaphysically and strictly, nothing is born or perishes, but all live ever in the Self). The resolute. determined, decided, un-wavering, doubt-free intelligence is single-minded. One-pointed, firm-based on the indubitable One. He who has this Right Understanding is able to escape from the binding chain of helpless unconscious births and deaths and rebirths (which chain is constituted by personal duty-less passions and emotions). Such a one goes to the Place of Peace. The Understanding becomes steady and sure when the mind is placid, undisturbed by loves and hates and derivative emotions. In the absence of concentrated attention upon the ultimate problems of life, upon the Nature of the Self, there can be no right Understanding, no peace of mind, no happiness. When the Understanding wades out of the marshes of infatuation with the things of sense, then is it able to cast off the glamor, the misleading will-o'-the-wisps, of traditions that have lost vitality, of 'hearsay' -*shruti* from which all living meaning has departed, of beliefs and rituals that are as atrophied vestiges; and then is the soul able to achieve steadfast vision of, and union with, the One Self. He who has cast off all selfish separative desire, all personal lusts and hates and fears and greeds, who remains undepressed in misfortune and sorrow, and unelated in success and joy, ever content, ever steadfastly established in the Universal Self, he is the man of Steady Understanding, of Assured Intelligence. Higher than the senses is Manas; higher than Manas is Buddhi; higher than Buddhi is Atma. He who has undestood That which is beyond Understanding, he is able to conquer that almost unconquerable foe, Kama, Desire. He who sees action in inaction and inaction in action, good in evil and evil in good, pleasure in pain and pain in pleasure, who sees all opposites balancing each other in the Pastime and Drama of the World-Process, the Play of the One Self, he has achieved the Right Understanding; his enterprises are unmotived by personal desire; his actions are sterilised by the fire of Self-knowledge and can no more bud out into bonds for his soul. The Sacrifice, the 'good-work,' of Knowledge is better than the sacri-fices of material things; all actions end in and with Right Knowledge. That Knowledge prevents the soul from falling into the power of worldly infatuations again; it enables the man to see all things and beings in the Atma, *i.e.*, in the I, in him-Self; it ferries him as in a boat across the waters of sin; it consumes the very seed of all selfish actions in him. There is no purifier of the soul like unto Right Knowledge; having achieved that Knowledge, the soul attains the Great Peace before long. That Absolute Happiness, beyond the reach of the senses, is comprehensible by the Understanding alone. Possessed of that subtle and utterly refined Understanding, guarding himself with fortitude from all contaminations, freed from sense of separate 'I' and 'mine,'[78] full of peace, the soul becometh ready for mergence into and identification with the Universal Self. The afflicted, the earnest enquirer, the ambitious, the wise possessed of knowledge—these four love Me, the I, devotedly; of them all, the knower, ever bearing Me, the I, in mind, single-heartedly devoted to the One Self in all beings, is the dearest to the I, as the I is the dearest to him; the knower is verily Myself, and looks to no-other. The I is the Buddhi of those possessed of Buddhi; the I is the knowledge of those possessed of knowledge. The I imparts to those intent upon seeking out and finding the Self, that path of Understanding whereby they approach and obtain that Self. Such is the final secret; he who understands it, has the Right Understanding, he has fulfilled all duty, and done all he had to do. The

[78] अहंता, ममता, "I-ness," "mine-ness," are the essence of what western psychologists call egoism (or the instinct of self-preservation) and the "sense of property" (the acquisitive instinct); the psycho-analysts would call these the "ego-complex" and the "property-complex" (a sub-division under the "herd-complex"), perhaps.

knowledge that sees Unity in Diversity and Diversity in Unity—that is the *sattvika*, right and righteous, knowledge. The Understanding, Intelligence, Reason, Buddhi, that knows both Pursuit and Renunciation, Right and Wrong, Good and Evil, Fear and Fearlessness, Death and Immortality, Bondage and Freedom, Descent of Spirit into Matter and Reascent thereout—that Buddhi is the *sattvika*, perfect, Understanding. Doing all deeds, performing all duties, as coming from and inspired of and caused by the One Self, betake thyself to the Yoga of the Understanding, the Right Reason, and identify thy-self with the Universal Self. The happiness, the peace, that is bitter as venom at first (because it involves the rooting out of separative selfishness), that same is sweet as nectar afterwards (because of the gain of universality, infinity, immortality; 'he who giveth up his life shall gain it multiplied infinite-fold, and he who tries to save it shall lose it'); it is the *sattvika* bliss that is born when there is unveiled the radiance of Atma-Buddhi, when they become lucid and placid."[79] Such is the insistence of the *Gita* on Buddhi. In other parts of the *Maha-bharata* also, we find important statements regarding it. Thus

मनसश्चापि बुद्धेश्च ब्रूहि मे लक्षणं परं ।
एतदध्यात्मविदुषां परं कार्यं विधीयते ।।

[79] Atma and Buddhi are greatly emphasised in the earlier Theosophical literature as the seventh and sixth principles of the seven that make up man (*vide* the Index to *The Secret Doctrine* under these two words); the fifth is the Manas, the principle of separative individuality, finite limitation and manifestation of the Atma as Jiva, of Chit as Chitta. This Manas, freed from the grosser body, filled with the inspiration of Buddhi and Atma, becomes capable of various kinds and degrees of immortality. In the plainer words of ordinary psychology and philosophy, when an individual soul has

बुद्धिरात्मानुगास्तीव उत्पादेन विधीयते ।
तदाश्रिता हि सा ज्ञेया बुद्धिस्तस्यैषिणी भवेत् ॥
बुद्धिरुत्पद्यते कार्यान्मनस्तूत्पन्नमेव हि ।
बुद्धेर्गुणविधानेन मनस्तद्गुणवद्भवेत् ॥ *Vana-parva*, ch. 183.
बुद्धिरात्मा मनुष्यस्य बुद्धिरेवात्मनो गतिः ।
तिष्ठती पुरुषे बुद्धिस्त्रिषु भावेषु वर्त्तते ॥ *Shanti-parva*, ch. 254.

Yudhishthira asks the "Serpent" Nahusha :"What is the distinction between Manas and Buddhi? Discrimination between the two is said to be the last task of psychology." And the answer (obscurely-worded) seems to be: "Buddhi is the accompaniment, the vesture, of the Atma; rests on and in it, and always desires it, *i.e.*, its essence is Self-Consciousness, Consciousness of the Universal Self. In other words, it may be said to be the Supra-conscious Desire of the Self for It-Self, the Desire to maintain, feel, realise It-Self. It takes of the form of laws or principles (*vidhi*) in manifestation. Buddhi comes

---

advanced, in evolution, to the stage of perceiving that it is identical in essence with the Universal Self or Principle of Life and Consciousness, then it can by intense wish and will, prolong any particular form that it desires to assume or wear, for an indefinite period, *i.e.*, can immortalise itself, comparatively. This is the attainment of *mukti*, *nirvana*, "initiation," freedom from fetters, deliverance, emancipation (from bonds of the body and superstitions of the mind), etc.

As the *Gita* says (vi, 30),

यो मां पश्यति सर्वत्र सर्वं च मयि पश्यति ।
तस्याहं न प्रणश्यामि स च मे न प्रणश्यति ॥

"He who beholds the I everywhere, and everything in the I, the I never drops away from him, is never lost by him, and he never drops away from the I, is never lost."

into manifestation when there is an object to achieve (it discovers the means which will secure the end, it discloses the laws of nature, the utilisation of which will fulfil the purpose): Manas is the manifest (operant, active desire). The Buddhi imparts its quality (*sattvika* or *rajasa* or *tamasa*) to the Manas: Manas displays outwardly and objectively, the attribute which the Buddhi sub-consciously prescribes . . . The Buddhi is verily the Atma of the human being; it is the radiance, the activity of the Self, and also its goal and refuge and last resort. Dwelling in the Self, the Purusha, it threads together the three parts of time, past, present, and future: it runs through the three moods, *sattva*, *rajas*, *tamas*."

In the larger sense, as said before, Buddhi is the Supra-conscious Scheme of the beginningless and endless World-process eternally existent as an ever-complete whole in the Self. It is the Universal seed-store or *Principle*, in God's Nature, which appears, in manifestation, as pseudo-infinite separate yet inseparably connected, individual "minds," "manas"-es, *chitta-s*, with their triple functions, of cognition-desire-action (buddhi-ahamkara-manas) generally, and as "rational intelligence" (*buddhi*) specially. This Universal Mind, *Chit*, and the Individual Mind, *chit-ta*, may be said to correspond broadly with Sanchita Karma (the Totality of causes, the Avyakta, the Unconscious) and Prarabdha or Kriyamana Karma (causes in the course of being worked out in effects, Vyakta, Conscious), respectively.[80]

---

[80]Avyakta, the Unmanifest, Mahat, the Vast, Mahan-Atma, the Great-Soul or Over-Soul, the Supra-concious which is the cause of the manifest or conscious, कारणमस्त्यव्यक्तं (*Sankhya-karika*) of the Darshanas: Brahma, "that which expands," Vishnu, "that which

In the smaller and more specific sense, *buddhi* is the cognitional aspect and function of the mind, as distinguished from the emotional (or desiderative) and the volitional (or active) aspects and functions, respectively called *ahamkara* and *manas;* while the summation of the three is the jiva, the individual soul, which may also be called *chitta* (whose function may be said to be memory, the "collector of all experiences," the "re-collector," from *chi,* to gather, whence *Chit,* another name for the Universal Buddhi, the Storehouse of all. In the Universal Triad, Atma-Buddhi-Manas, Atma is the Universal Self, Buddhi is Universal Mind (including the three *Shaktis* of *jnana-ichchha-kriya,* all, corresponding to the Trinity and Vishnu-Shiva-Brahma), and Manas may be said to be the *Principle* of individuation, the seed of the This. The Manas of this larger Triad may

---

pervades," Shiva. "that which sleeps within," Savitri and Veda-mata, the Mother of the Vedas, Chitra-gupta, the Secret Picture. Radha-Durga, "the giver of joy and helper in difficulties," etc., of the Puranas: the Nous and Demiurgos of the Greeks; the Unconscious Will-and-Imagination of some modern western philosophers; Aql-i-kul, Total Intelligence, Aql-i-awwal. First Intelligence, Ruh-i-kul, Total Soul or Over-soul, Haqiqat-i-Muhammadi, the Glorious Truth. Ummul-kitab, the Mother of Scriptures. Lauh-i-Mahfuz, the Preserved or Hidden Tablet or Record. of the Sufis; the Holy Ghost and the Christ-Principle of the Christian Mystics and Gnostics: Smara-Kama Sankalpa (God's Memory-Desire-Ideation), Jagatprana, Anima Mundi. Sutratma, Over-soul, Common Sense, Public Opinion, Public Enthusiasm, etc.—all these seem to be only aspects of one and the same Buddhi, the Primal Radiance, of the Self. as light. heat, etc., aré of the Energy of the visible Sun. the physical counterpart of the Spiritual Sun.

For attempt to expound, in some detail, the meaning of Buddhi and Manas as Total Universal Ideation and Individual Mind, and also the special other meanings of these two words, the reader may refer to *The Science of Peace* and *The Pranava-Vada*.

be said to become, in the individual jiva, the particular triad of *buddhi-ahamkara-manas* or cognition-(egoistic) desire-action; these three may be said to be the reflections, as it were, of the larger three Buddhi-Atma-Manas. When the *sattva*-quality, the intellectual aspect of the individual soul, prevails, and is not overpowered or greatly tainted or influenced by the lower *tamas* and *rajas*, selfish desire and selfish activity, but is influenced by the higher *tamas* and *rajas* of sympathetic, compassionate, unselfish desire and philanthropic activity for the good of all, then the individual *buddhi* comes into *rapport* with, opens out to the inflow, as it were, of the Universal Buddhi; and as the deliberate refinement and the consciously unselfish philanthropy of the individual grow, so more and more of the infinite knowledge and powers contained in the Universal Buddhi flow into it, directly, as well as through the spiritual Hierarchy of gods and rshis—so the traditions indicate.[81]

It is this Universal Buddhi, this first form of the formless Prakrti of Purusha, the Nature of the Self, which is invoked in the Gayatrimantra, which the Manu enjoins upon all his children to recite, more mentally than audibly, day after day, if they would not fall from their status of twice-born, regenerate, Aryan. "May the effulgent radiance of the Universal Spirit, the Father of All, illuminate, inspire, guide our *Intelligence*." "The Aryan may or may not perform any other religious rite, if he but accomplish this meditation regularly," says Manu. For, even obviously, if the understanding sees and acts rightly, all the life will go right; if it goes wrongly, all goes wrong. Krishna

---

[81]See *The Secret Doctrine*, I, PP. 153-157, and other pages (per Index), *re* Buddhi and Manas; and the *Pranava-Vada*.

declares the same fact when he says that man should seek and find refuge in right understanding, in Reason ; and that he who loses Reason, loses himself.

Yet such is the degeneration of the so-called "re-generates," the "twice-born," to-day, that their most "learned" and most influential "custodians of Dharma" are not ashamed, and do not hesitate, to proclaim loudly that "Reason has no place in Dharma". The history of all religions shows the same corruption, the same rapid downfall from enlightenment of the understanding into the dark-ness of blind faith and unquestioning obedience. The founders of new religions, or, rather, the reformers of deformed religion, the genuine lovers, helpers, servers of mankind, have always tried to inculcate Self-knowledge, whence Self-respect, Self-reliance, Self-control, Self-government; for political Self-government is not possible without spiritual Self-knowledge inasmuch as true political self-government means government, *i.e.*, legislation, which is the essence of government, by the higher self of the People, their best and wisest, their most experienced, most philanthropic, most selfless, most self-governed, self-controlled, Self-knowing, select and elect; and such self-government is possible only to a people among whom Self-knowledge is possessed by a fair proportion, and is honored by the majority. The kingdom of heaven on earth, in plain words, is legislation and rule by the wise and philanthropic. Hence the religious reformers, by endeavoring to spread Self-knowledge, directly help to establish the kingdom of heaven on earth. But the after-comers, hypnotising vampires and soul-suckers, have equally invariably again deformed the religoins, and misled human beings into *other*-worship and *other*-dependence. As the Upanishat says, "What the gods created, the demons ran after and touched and tainted with Sin".[82] The Self is always being defeated by selfishness; Brahman by Maya, Its own Maya; God by Satan; benevolence by malevolence; wise science by cunning ignorance; humanitarianism by sectarianism; all-inclusive tolerance by all-exclusive bigotry. So that the Play may never cease, Eternal Truth is inseparably conjoined with Everlasting Falsehood; Avidya is the twin sister of Vidya.[83]

See. It should be fairly clear from what has been said above that the *Gita* is one long hymn in praise of Atma-Buddhi, of that Self-lightened Wisdom which in daily use, manifests, or should manifest, as enlightened rational self-reliance. Yet the one line of the *Gita* which comes most readily and frequently to the lips of the "learned", the Pandits, when they wish to stifle inconvenient criticism of the current perverse and pernicious ways of what is known as "Hinduism," is this,

तस्माच्छास्त्रं प्रमाणं ते कार्याकार्यव्यवस्थितौ ।

"The *shastra* (some written book), is the law for you as to what to do or not do." One is reminded of the English saying: "The devil can quote the Bible for his own purposes." All the rest of the *Gita* is ignored, the immediate context of the line is thrust aside, a "half-truth," a half-sentence, a half-thought, is put forward as the whole truth.

Because of its " practical" importance, the subject deserves to be dwelt on for a while. The word *shastra* is used by

---

[82]यद् देवा अकुर्वंस्तद्दैत्या अभ्यद्रवन्स्तत्पाप्मना अस्पृशन् ।

[83]See, for illustration, the chapters on the birth and growth of Christianity and Islam in such a well-known book as Gibbon's *Roman Empire.*

Krishna four times[83a] in the course of the *Gita*; three times in xvi, 23-24, out of which the line above-quoted is taken; and once in xv, 20. The "whole truth," which Krishna declares, is this: " Who flings aside the rules of conduct enjoined by *shastra*, and indulges his desires wilfully, he attains not *siddhi* (accomplishment, perfection), nor happiness nor the highest goal. Therefore let the *shastra* be thy authority, in determining what to do and what to avoid. Having *known* ( *carefully ascertained* ) what the *shastra*-law says, do thy work in this world." What does Krishna mean by *shastra*? He explains it himself, shortly before, in xv,20: "Thus have I expounded to thee, the deepest, the most secret, *shastra*," *i.e.*, the Science of the Infinite, the Universal, Highest, Best Self, Purushottama, Paramatma. Does the ordinary theologian-pandit understand and mean the same thing by that word, when he quotes the half-verse, to gag his rationalist questioner? Not at all. He means any one of a thousand pen-and-ink concoctions in Samskrt verse or prose, by mediaeval and subsequent theologian-pandits, dealing mostly with the most trumpery and trifling matters of ritualistic detail (which Krishna has censured so strongly in the second chapter), and professing to be based, if at all, on some "letter, which killeth, of the Bible" (some Smrti or Purana text in this case), dragged away from its context and its right meaning. All the most important and significant words of the ancient Samskrt texts, which have a perpetual bearing on the daily life of the individual and of Society, have been similarly deprived of their rightful meaning and stuffed with wrong ones instead, whereby the whole of that individual and social life has been perverted.

---

83a. See the Word-Index in the *Gita*, by Annie Besant and Bhagavan Das.

Thus, to take another and very important instance, Krishna expressly declares that "The system of the four orders of vocations or classes (now called caste) has been produced by the (very Nature of the ) Self, in accordance with the characteristic qualities and the temperamental functions of individuals, for the due division of (the social) labor, a division made in assonance with the predominant characteristics of (psycho-physical) Nature."

चातुर्वर्ण्यं मया सृष्टं गुणकर्मविभागशः ।। iv, 13.
कर्माणि प्रविभक्तानि स्वभावप्रभवैर्गुणैः ।। xviii, 41.

He does not mention heredity at all in this connection; yet, for centuries now, under theologian regime, "heredity," "birth," has been the one sole determining factor in the so-called Hindu caste-system, to the utter exclusion of "spontaneous variation". And the result is that, instead of complete socio-economico-political organisation, the one sole purpose of the "vocation" -system, there is utter disorganisation in Hindu Society to-day. More will be said about this later on. In the meanwhile, the discussion of the important word *shastra* may be closed with a verse or two from *Manu*, to supplement the quotations from the *Gita*.

प्रत्यक्षं चानुमानं च शास्त्रं च विविधागमम् ।
त्रयं सुविदितं कार्यं धर्मशुद्धिमभीप्सता ।।
आर्षं धर्मोपदेशं च वेदशास्त्राविरोधिना ।
यस्तर्केणानुसंधत्ते स धर्मं वेद नेतरः ।। xii, 105-6.
न ह्यनध्यात्मवित् कश्चित् क्रियाफलमुपाश्नुते ।। vi, 82.

"He who desires purity in and of law ( would make good laws and would interpret and observe laws well and rightly, correctly), he must possess in fullness these three: (1) first-hand direct observation and experience, (2) argument, (3) science in its many branches, the body of knowledge which (has been accumulated by the labors of previous generations and) has 'come down' (*agama*) from the past. He who livingly interprets the laws counselled by the Rshis, in accordance with the science of the Infinite Self (*Veda-shastra, Veda-anta, Adhyatma-shastra*, the Crown and Finality of knowledge), in the light of reason and argument, only he understands the Dharma-law, and none else. He who does not know the Science of the Self (psychology and meta-physic, which is the master co-ordinator of all the other sciences), he cannot secure right fruit from any action."

Even if the word *shastra* should be taken in its lower narrower sense, of some particular text-book, even so Krishna's words, "Having *known*, *i.e.*, carefully ascertained, what the *shastra*-law says," cannot be escaped from. Granted that *shastra* is the authority, who and how to decide whenever this text is *shastra* or is not *shastra*, is good and true *shastra* or is bad and false *shastra*? Even after deciding that it is good and true *shastra*, who and how to decide what this text means, whether this is the meaning, or this else? Is the Veda to be believed, or the Bible, or the Quran; is Manu to be followed, or Rama, or Krishna, or Vyasa, or Zoroaster, or Moses, or Christ, or Muhammad, or any other? Who is to decide, who does actually decide daily, for me, except my-Self, ultimately—as the thousands of conversions from one religion to another daily irrefutably prove? Even the most uneducated, the most illiterate, has this indefeasible might of Atma-Buddhi potential in him, whereby, whatever the outer superficial motives may be, he sits in judgment between and over the highest, and decides as he thinks fit. "That the intellect cannot go farther, that reason fails, that thought cannot climb higher— this too is the decision of intellect, reason, thought itself."[84]

Much greater is the self-dependence in the case of one who has achieved Atma-Buddhi consciously, and for whom, therefore, "nothing more remains to do or to seek after, except to keep the Wheel of Life and Law turning and seek the happiness of self in and through the happiness of all selves, so far as may be." (*Gita*, xv—20; iii, 16-18.)

The soul that has thus attained majority by achieving Self-knowledge, is able to stand on its own feet, in joy and in sorrow, in peace and in war, and inwardly feel it all as Pastime and Drama, Lila, while it performs, at the same time, the duties attaching to its body, its material vesture, with an even mind, and endeavors, to the best of its ability, to lead other souls to the same majority.

अच्छेद्योऽयमदाह्योऽयमक्लेद्योऽशोष्य एव च ।
नित्यः सर्वगतः स्थाणुरचलोऽयं सनातनः ।।
आत्मन्येवात्मना तुष्टः स्थितप्रज्ञः स उच्यते ।। ii, 24, 55.
यस्त्वात्मरतिरेव स्यादात्मतृप्तश्च मानवः ।
आत्मन्येव च संतुष्टस्तस्य कार्यं न विद्यते ।। iii, 17.
योगयुक्तो विशुद्धात्मा विजितात्मा जितेन्द्रियः ।
सर्वभूतात्मभूतात्मा कुर्वन्नपि न लिप्यते ।।
स्थिरबुद्धिरसंमूढो ब्रह्मविद्ब्रह्मणि स्थितः ।
स ब्रह्मयोगयुक्तात्मा सुखमक्षय्यमश्नुते ।। v, 7, 20, 21.

---

[84] न बुद्धिरस्तीत्यपि बुद्धिसाध्यं। विचारस्य खंडनमपि विचारेणैव क्रियते ।
See note at the end of Ch. xvi, in Annie Besant and Bhagavandas's *Gita*.

उद्धरेदात्मनात्मानं नात्मानमवसादयेत् ।
आत्मैव ह्यात्मनो बंधुरात्मैव रिपुरात्मनः ।।
यत्र चैवात्मनात्मानं पश्यन्नात्मनि तुष्यति ।
यं लब्ध्वा चापरं लाभं मन्यते नाधिकं ततः ।
तं विद्याद्दुःखसंयोगवियोगं दुःखसंज्ञितम् ।। vi. 5, 20-23.
ध्यानेनात्मनि पश्यन्ति केचिदात्मानमात्मना ।
यः पश्यति तथात्मानमकर्त्तारं स पश्यति ।। xiii, 24-29.
आत्मैव देवताः सर्वाः सर्वमात्मन्यवस्थितं ।
आत्मा हि जनयत्येषां कर्मयोगं शरीरिणाम् ।।
सर्वमात्मनि संपश्येत्सच्चासच्च समाहितः ।
सर्वमात्मनि संपश्यन्नाधर्मे कुरुते मनः ।।
सर्वभूतेषु चात्मानं सर्वभूतानि चात्मनि ।
समं पश्यन्नात्मयाजी स्वाराज्यमधिगच्छति ।।
एवं यः सर्वभूतेषु पश्यत्यात्मानमात्मना ।
स सर्वसमतामेत्य ब्रह्माभ्येति परं पदम् ।। (*Manu*, xii. 91-125.)

"Realise that the Self in all, the Self of All, my-Self, thy-Self, him-Self, our-self is deathless, immortal, eternal, Sanatana. Because the Self is Sanatana, therefore the Dharma, the Code of Life, which is based upon It, which flows from the principles, the facts and laws, of Its Nature, is Sanatana Dharma, the Eternal Law. He who has found, and rests in, him-Self, peaceful, content, controlled of sense, steady, he has found the everlasting happiness. Uplift the self by the Self, allow not the self to be depressed; the Self is the friend of the self, the self is the foe of the Self; the Self is its own friend and its own enemy; there is no other friend or foe. No greater gain is there than the gain of the Self, which, actionless, causes all action. The Self is all the gods;

all is in the Self; all the forms and all their activities, which make up the World and its incessant process, are the work of the Self. Behold all good and all evil, all truth and all falsehood, with deep inner vision, in thy-Self; he who seeth thus, he avoideth all sinful ways. He who sees all things in the Self, and the Self in all things, he achieves same-sightedness, he realises the law of analogy, he sees the same laws working everywhere, he attains Self-government, the Empire of the Self, the state of Supreme Brahman."

Such is the utterly rationalist, incontrovertible, Self-dependence that is taught by the *Gita*. And what for? For purposes of vague, mystical, emotional, sentimental enjoyment? No; but for the uses of familiar everyday life, as well as of great occasions of "practical" difficulty and importance, of profound heart-searching and mind-disturbance, such as that which oppressed Arjuna's soul when he found himself facing his nearest kith and kin for battle to the death. The teaching of the *Gita* is not only deeply rationalist but very pragmatic, very practical. Its metaphysic and psychology are all intended to be brought to bear on every question in hand, smallest or largest, lowest or highest, for all are governed by the same laws, the law of analogy, as said above. The so-called "mystical," "superphysical," etc., may belong to different planes of matter, and may be unfamiliar, but that does not make it any more wonderful, more unintelligible, more awe-inspiring, than the most familiar.

The question is sometimes asked, Why, when the simple point in issue is, "To fight or not to fight," should the *Gita* refer encyclopaedically to all things in heaven and earth, as it does? Is it all relevant? The answer is that a part cannot be understood except in relation to other parts; that in order to understand any one part fully and properly, you must understand all the other parts also, of the whole: that the clearer the knowledge is of the other parts, the fuller and deeper will be the knowledge of the one part; but that inasmuch as such omniscience is obviously impossible to any limited individual, however highly progressed, at least a general knowledge of the outlines of the whole is indispensable for the special knowledge of any one particular part. This is only another aspect of the idea embodied in the well-known definition of culture, *viz*,. to know something of everything and everything of some one thing. When the question involved is the ethical one of duty, obviously no solution is possible without scrutiny of the component elements of the situation, out of and in which the question has arisen, of all the persons as between whom the duty is felt or alleged to arise, as due from one or more to another or others. It is not without strong reason in the very nature of things, that the so-called "human" sciences, psychology (or rather, psycho-physics, the science of human nature), logic (the science of right thinking), ethics (the science of right desiring and right acting), sociology (including economics, politics, civics, etc., as the science of right social organisation) are generally put into one group instinctively by educators, in the West, also; while metaphysic co-ordinates them all, as well as the so-called "material" sciences grouped mainly under Physics and Chemistry, with Biology coming between the two groups.[55] In the Samskrit classification of sciences, as the Shastras of (1) Dharma, (2) Artha, (3) Kama, and (4) Moksha or Darshana, the subor-

[55]See J.A.Thomson, *Introduction to Science* (Home University Library), pp. 47, 106, 166, 167, 251.

dination of all to the Principle of Life and Consciousness, the Self, is much more explicit, and all the details are grouped around the life of man as their centre and as the object of their subservience. No problem of human life and ethics can be solved adequately, therefore, without sociological and psychological considerations, and the help of metaphysical principles; just as no geometrical proposition can be worked out without constant reference to the definitions, axioms, postulates. Indeed, in Indian thought, Dharma (ethics, politics, law, etc.,) is clearly regarded as "applied" metaphysic and "applied" psychology, in the same way as a particular art or craft is "applied" particular science. To find out "What is my duty?" I must first find out "What am I, whence, where, whither, how, why?"

To convince Arjuna that it is his duty to do battle, even unto death, against the usurpers of Yudhisthira's birth-right and birth-duty, it is necessary to give him an idea of the nature and organisation of human society and the relations of human beings to one another; to make that clear, again, the nature of the human being and of his life, here as well as herebefore and hereafter, has to be stated; that, in turn, for elucidation, requires an at least rapid exposition of the nature of the whole World-process, *i.e.*, of the relation of Spirit and Matter. Thus has a question of ethics to be solved—solved finally and conclusively, that is, and not merely touched superficially—by going to the root of the matter, with the help of fundamental metaphysics, and is not possible to solve otherwise.[56] The "practical" conclusion of the whole seven hundred verses of universe-ranging "argument" is: "Therefore fight, O Arjuna!"[57]

---

[56] See, in Annie Besant and Bhagavan Das's *Bhagavad-Gita*, the "Contents (setting forth the Argument of the *Gita*)".

[57] तस्माद् युध्यस्व भारत ।

Because of the need to go to the fundamental universals, for conclusive decisions of human, and, indeed, all, problems, does Krishna, laying strees on Buddhi, Rational Intelligence, throughout his discourse, take care to state that the perfect, *sattvika*, Buddhi is that which knows the whole history of the Pursuit of and entrance into Matter by Spirit, and also of the Renunciatian and emergence out of Matter by Spirit, *i.e.*, knows the whole Nature of the Self, the whole World-process.

The "axioms," by the diligent application of which such Buddhi is able to reconcile conflicting views, the proverbial two sides of every question, and to arrive at the golden mean, the right middle course, in all difficult situations, may be briefly gathered here. "The I is all; there is Naught-Else. All is in the I; therefore all is everywhere and always. The World-process is made up of pairs of equal opposites. Things are named after their predominant characteristic. Views change with viewpoints. Laws, rights-and-duties, differ with time-place-and-circumstance. Truth is in the mean, error in the extreme. The limited is the relative; therefore statements regarding the limited can be, must be, relative only, comparative only, always."[88]

If it be desired to compress the whole teaching of the *Gita* into the smallest possible compass, we have it done for us already in a quarter-verse, of just four words:

---

[88]अहमेव, न मत्तोऽन्यत् । मत्तः परतरं नान्यत् । वासुदेवः सर्वमिति । मयि सर्वमिदं प्रोतं । सर्वं सर्वत्र सर्वदा । द्वंद्वमयः संसारः । वैशेष्यात्तु तद्वादस्तद्वादः । प्रस्थानभेदाद् दर्शनभेदः । देशकालनिमित्तानां भेदैर्धर्मो विभिद्यते । अधिकारिभेदाद् धर्मभेदः । आश्रयेत् मध्यमां वृत्तिमति सर्वत्र वर्जयेत् । परिमितं सापेक्षं । विभज्य वचनीयं ।

मामनुस्मर युध्य च । viii, 7.

"Remember Me and fight."

To ever bear the higher Self in mind, is to have achieved the essence of that higher Reason which is the wisest counsellor and the strongest ally in the battle of life. Know your-Self to be immortal; so knowing, no fear can assail you; stand on your own feet, then, firmly; help others, instead of requiring to be helped; do not fall prostrate in blind worship before idols of your own creation, whether physical or super-physical, mystical or intellectual, scriptural or any other; do not allow yourself to be led astray by mere mysterious words and sensationalist hopes held out in vague languge, half revealing, half concealing, of ritualistic ceremonies and references to Scripture; ascertain your duty, independently, in the light of Self-knowledge; within you is the Light of the Universe; nothing that is outside of you can help you; you are, the Self is, the I is, I am, in the last resort, the sole judge between gods and idols, between prophets and world-teachers and religion-founders and avataras; between all Scriptures and all creeds; you are, the I is, I am, the maker and container of all these."[9]

---

[9]Some Persian Sufi verses, and their equivalents in Samskrt and English, deserve to be recorded here, as pithily summing up the argument which irrefutably estabishes the supremacy of the Self.

Zan ki usta ra shinasa ham tu i.
Jumla usta ra khud usta ham tu i.
Chun haqiqat ra muhaqqiq khud tu i.
Ain haq in-ast Ain-ul-Haq tu i.
Hastiye Rab ra mujawwiz chun tu i.
B-il yaqin Allahu-Akbar khud tu i.

In the quarter-verse quoted, *Mam*, "Me," is the Supreme Self; *anu*, "following after," "constantly", "faithfully," indicates devotion; *smara*, "remember," ""memory," the foundation of reasoning, the Reason which is based upon,

---

गुरोर्योग्यत्वविज्ञाता त्वं, नतोऽसि गुरोर्गुरुः ।
सत्यासत्यविनिश्चेता त्वं, नतोऽसि मतोऽपि मत् ।
ईश्वरास्तित्वनिर्णेता त्वं, नतोऽसि परेश्वर : ॥

Since thou decidest who is fit to take
Or not to take for Teacher, thou thy-Self
Must, surely, than all Teachers wiser be.
Since thou dost judge that this is True, this not,
Maker of Truth, most True, thy-Self must be.
Since thou determinest whether God is,
Or is not, surely thine own Self must be
The inmost being of Godhead, Greatest God.

The truth that man is himself the embodiment of Atma-Buddhi, is his own God and the Source of all Wisdom and Scripture, if he would but so recognise himself, and become *insan-ul-kamil* or *mard-i-tamam, maryada-purusha, jivan-mukta*, "the perfect man. " and the greater truth that it is the duty of such "perfect man" to serve the world and help in turning the wheel of samsara, are well put in some Sufi verses:

Dar haqiqat khud tu i Ummu-l-kitab;
Khud ze khud ayat-i-khud ra baz yab.
Lauh-i-Mahfuz ast dar maani dil-at;
Har che min khwahi shawad z-u hasil-at,
Kase mard-e-tamam ast az tamami,
Kunad ba khwajagi kar-e ghulami.

That is:

Thyself the Parent of all Scriptures thou!
All God-spell thine own heart will give enow.
The Secret Sacred Record is thy heart;
Whate'er thou wishest, ask; it will impart.
Rare is the soul that being Master braves
The noble task of slaving for the slaves.

follows after, is the radiance of, the Self, indicates knowledge; *yudhya*, "fight," indicates action. Thus this little text sums up the whole of "practical mysticism," philosophical ethics, combination of the three paths of knowledge, devotion, and action: Wage the battle of life, carry on the World-Drama of love and war, life and death, in subservience to and in accordance with devoted and incessant recollection of the Self.

## The Practical Devotionalism of the Gita

The *loka-sangraha* or social organisation, referred to above, in the setting of which human rights-and-duties arise, and which Krishna incarnated to restore, by breaking the excessive militarism which was disturbing it, may be dealt with in a little more detail. But before this is done, a few words should be said about another aspect of the *Gita*.

It is a text-book of Spiritual Rationalism, in the first degree, and as natural issue therefrom, of Rational Practicalism, in the second degree, no doubt. But it is also a manual of Practial Devotionalism in the third degree. It supplies meat for the strong. But it also provides milk for babes. The parents of a family exhort the grown-up juniors, who are on the point of attaining majority, to stand on their own feet now, begin to share the family burdens, and give the elders some relief. But they also continue to feed and help in every way the smaller boys and girls and children and infants. The infants need to be nursed and wholly carried in the arms; the toddling children to be supported with a finger, which they, in turn, clutch strongly; the boys and girls, to be kept within easy reach of help, and put to school-work of various kinds; the adolescent youths and maidens, to be given appropriate advice, and watched from a distance, while at college or doing apprenticeship of one kind or another: the fully grown-up, the adult, to be gladly allowed if energetic and willing, encouraged if shy, or, if they are lazy or lacking in self-reliance and will, to be insistently forced, to look after themselves, in the first place, and, in the second, to help in the work of reading the still younger generation, 'keep the wheel of life and law turning,'[90] and illustrate, in the small human joint family, the ideal principle of managing the world-family, the principle which is the foundation of *loka-sangraha*, "From all according to their capacities, to all according to their needs" (with comforts and even luxuries, besides, in the shape of public possessions common to all).

As the small, so the great. So says the law of analogy, *sama-darshita*, same-sightedness. The vision which discerns the same law operating equally everywhere, on all scales, atomic and starry, in all organisms, in all departments of the World-process, in all times and places—that is *sama-darshita*. As the small single human family of a human parent, as the larger nation-family of the patriarch-king-priest, the perpetual Sovereign Legislature-Executive, so is a great World-family, it would seem, of the Spiritual Hierarchy and its Chief. President,[91] or Ishwara. The motive which inspires Ishwaras, which is their main interest in life, is, as said before,[92] the compassionate yearning to help souls across the profound chaos of *kalpa-pralayas* and *maha pralayas*, by enabling them to find the path of rectitude and the final knowledge of the Self.[93]

---

[90]*Gita* iii, 16.

[91]The *Bhavishya Purana* tells how in one *kalpa*-eon Vishnu occupies the *Purana-purush-asanam*."the seat of the Eldest" among Elders, the first among equals; in another, Saraswati; in another, Varuna; and so on.

[92]P.76 *supra*.

[93]तस्य (ईश्वरस्य) आत्मानुग्रहाभावेऽपि भूतानुग्रहः प्रयोजनम्, ज्ञानधर्मोपदेशेन कल्पप्रलयमहाप्रलयेषु संसारिणः पुरुषानुद्धरिष्यामीति ।

*Yoga-bhashya*, i, 25.

It should be borne in mind, here, that though the Ultimate Truth is very simple, very quiet and peaceful, very familiar, "nearer than hands and feet," our very Self, yet, to realise it, myriad errings away from it, deep forgettings of it, countless joys and sorrowings, experiences of sharp pleasures and pains, of ecstasies of bliss and woes beyond words, deeps of chaos, turmoils of cosmos (all made up of and by Will-and-Imagination), have to be passed through. To attain majority, to stand on one's own feet, feels simple enough when that state has been achieved; but how many helplessnesses and illnesses of infancy, childhood, youth, requiring constant

---

Compare the *maha-karuna* of the "Buddhas of Compassion." The subtle and "mystical" differences and distinctions between the Bhakta-s and the Jnani-s, the Vishishtadvaiti-s and the Advaiti-s, the Buddhists and the Jainas, and, again, between the Buddhas and Pratyeka-buddhas, the Maha-yanists and the Hina-yanists, the Shvetambara Jainas and the Digambara Jainas, etc., or the philosophers of perpetual Progressive Change and the philosophers of Changelessness, may, perhaps, in one way, be brought home, and made more plain, and reconciled, by the familiar analogy of the distinction between the same grown-up person (1) in his relation to his children, and (2) in his relation to other grown-up persons of other families. To realise the aptness of the illustration, consider the belief, expressed in some works of Theosophical literature, that the anniversary of Gautama Buddha's Enlightenment, his attainment of the wisdom and the peace of Nirvana, is celebrated annually by the members of the Spiritual Hierarchy of the Earth, in a retired spot in Thibet, on the full moon night of the month of Vaishakha (generally May) and the Bodhisattva, officiating on the occasion, recites, as principal part of the ceremony, the "Maha-mangala Sutta" which was uttered by the Buddha when some angels questioned him as to what was the Greatest Blessing. This noble sermon is, in the first place, a eulogy of the virtuous and happy family in which all the members are inspired by affection for each other and by dutiful righteousness in dealings with others; and, in the second place, of the realisation of Nirvana. In the words of Manu, we would say that the greatest blessing was the fulfilment of the duties of the four ashramas, or stages of life, the first two covering life in the world, and the last two, life

and anxious care on the part of the elders, have to be undergone, before it is achieved ! As is the maturing of the physical body, so is that of the psychical, superphysical, emotional-intellectual body. Often a whole long and serious illness, a prostrating emotional shock, has to be undergone, and undergone repeatedly, before a fact or law of life is clearly understood and becomes lastingly and usefully engraved on the memory. Extreme elations and depressions, agonies of strenuous thinking, intellectual and emotional wrestlings with doubts and despairs, wih angels and devils, inner and outer, in life-and-death grapples, have to be passed through, before the simple fact is realised that all the World-process is *in* the Self, as the ecstatic heavens and the nightmare hells of the dream are

---

out of it, i.e., the realisation of Nirvana. Love one another, help each other, as purely, as unselfishly, as possible. and do your duty, realising that the Self in each and all is Eternal—this seems to be the whole of Spritual Ethics, for all worlds and planes: this seems to be the sum and substance of the counsel of all the lovers and well-wishers of the Great Family of the whole Human Race; whether it be put in language, distant, elusive, gorgeously colored. "mystical," like the clouds of sunset and sunrise, or in words simple and near and clear as crystal drops of water, which are the precipitate, and also the origin, and contain all the essence of all those clouds.

This divine compassion and sweet family affection, too, are, no doubt, Maya-Illusion, Imagination, Ideation ; but they are the maternal, the finest, sublimest, most glorious, aspect of it. In order to reconcile Maha-yana and Hina-yana, we may interpret the former as Maha-karuna-yana, the Path of Great Compassion, the higher Bhakti-marga, for purposes of *practical* conduct, to help others, so long as the soul continues to wear a separate individual body of any sort or plane ; and we may understand the latter as Sanga-hina-yana, the Path of Freedom from Attachment and clinging to any particular thing or separate personality, the Jnana-marga, for purposes of *theoretical* understanding. The two are not separate or incompatible, but, rather, aspects of the same ; as the maternal and the

all in the awakened dreamer.[94] During such passing through and maturation, the elder souls have to brood over the younger.

Therefore, for such younger souls, Krishna's Aham, "I", means, not so much the Impersonal, "All-personal," Universal I, as his grand and glorious particular personality. "Tie your souls to him, with the strong bonds of friendship, affection, love, devoted worship"; to him, or to any other extraordinary personality, of similar well-proven quality, like the founders of the great religions, Buddha, Jesus, Muhammad,

paternal ; as the outer, for the purpose of serving others, and the inner, for purposes of self-reliance, consolation, fortitude. Individuals may show one or the other aspect predominantly, and be able all the more and better to co-operate with and supplement each other. Nursery tales of Northern India say that Gauri-Parvati and Shiva-Shankara (Prana and Buddhi, Heart and Head, Emotion and Wisdom, Power and Peace, star-spangled Light and profound Firmament) wander abroad every night, mounted on the four-legged Bull (the Dharma-megha Vrsha, the four-quartered Space which rains, *varshati, mehati,* the *dharma-s,* the Laws of Nature), from World to World. And always She stops over some crying child or wailing woman or sobbing man, and begs Him hard to change the tears to smiles. And always He tries to remonstrate and demonstrate to Her the wisdom of the Laws, and that if She would but let alone, the tears would shortly expiate the sins and bring release. And always His expostulations go in vain, and She grows lachrymose Herself. And so perforce He has to change the tears to smiles, and give what the weeper wants. And the accounts are lengthened, and more births and rebirths caused, and more scenes and acts added to the ever-lengthening Drama. Thus She and He co-operate with Their different temperaments to keep revolving the Universal Wheel of Life which is always trying to defy and flout the Law, and of Law which is always reasserting itself over Life.

[94] *Gita*, vi, 45; vii, 3, 19.

etc., or any divine ideal (embodied in a god or demi-god of the various pantheons, an avatara,[95] or in one of the "thousand" or "hundred" names of Shiva or Vishnu or Allah), who may appeal to your imagination, sentiment, intelligence, aspirations, in your special stage of evolution.

In this, his personal, aspect—but the Impersonal One is also peeping out from behind it quite visibly all the time—Krishna holds out such winning temptations to coax souls to come to him—even as a mother to children!

पत्रं पुष्पं फलं तोयं यो मे भक्त्या प्रयच्छति ।
तदहं भक्त्युपहृतमश्नामि प्रयतात्मनः ॥
अनन्याश्चिन्तयंतो मां ये जनाः पर्युपासते ।
तेषां नित्याभियुक्तानां योगक्षेमं वहाम्यहम् ॥ ix, 22, 25.

"Bring me only a fresh leaf, a new flower, a ripe fruit, only a little limpid water—and offer it to me with love and devotion. Make the offering of love with a pure heart; and I will accept it with joy. And, in return, I will undertake wholly the protection, and the promotion of the welfare, of such a soul; the soul has only to be single-minded, ever-devoted, ever-loyal, and think of only Me-not-another, and keep ever close to me (*an-anya*,[96] *pary-upasate*)". "It is so easy to please Me, and win my permanent and complete favor, and

---

[95]From *ava*, down, and *tr*, to float across; a being descending (from the Sun). *Hulul* seems to be the Sufi word for *avatara*; also *mazhar*, manifestation; qurb-i-farayiz, qurb-i-nawafil, etc., seem to express kinds and degrees.

[96]I have referred, in a previous foot-note, to my recently published Hindi book, *Samanvaya*. In the last chapter of that book, I have gathered together a number of Samskrt texts, from the old books, which support the Logion, "I-This (=Another)-Not," expounded in *The Science of Peace*,

all the wealth of all the worlds which that favor means," he seems to say; "I want so very little service!" Is he not very simple-hearted, so easily propitiated? But underneath this seeming guilelessness, the Lord is very deep and very artful! Do you not see that, pretending to ask nothing, he has asked for the very quintessence of all the beauty and all the vitality of the universe ? What is more fascinating than new leaf and fresh flower, more healthful than sweet fruit and crystal water? "Behold the lilies of the valley; not Solomon in all his glory was more gorgeously arrayed than they." And more; it is by no means true that he is content with even these, and wants nothing more! He wants what is much more than these. He wants the *whole* love of the *whole* soul! He mentions

---

and the *Pranavavada*, and which I came across in the course of readings subsequent to the publication of the second edition of *The Science of Peace*. I give here, two more texts, discovered after the publication of *Samanvaya* (*i.e.*, "Synthesis").

Sanat-Kumara says to one of the Rudra-s ;

मोऽहमेव न मेऽन्योऽस्ति य एवमभिमन्यते ।<br>
न मन्यते ममान्योऽस्ति येन चेतोऽस्म्यचेतनः ॥<br>
एवमेवाभिमन्येत बुध्यमानोऽप्यनात्मवान् ।<br>
अहमेव न मेऽन्योऽस्ति न प्रबुद्धवशानुगः ॥<br>
अव्यक्तस्थो गुणानेष नित्यमेवाभिमन्यते ॥

*Maha-bharata*, Anushasana-parva, Ch. 168.

And the *Varaha-Upanishat* says :

अहमेव सुखं नान्यदन्यच्चेन्नैव तत्सुखम् । Chap. 2,v.7.

The significance of the *Gita*-verse, vi, 25, may also be pondered in this connection.

आत्मसंस्थं मनः कृत्वा न किंचिदपि चिंतयेत् ।<br>
. *e.*, आत्मा ( अहम् ) किंचित् ( आत्मनः अन्यत् किंचित् ) न, इति चिंतयेत्.

*Bhagavata*, XI, xiv, 44 is to the same effect.

leaf and flower and fruit and water only once; but of love he is so insatiable that he mentions it twice; and not satisfied with even that, he adds, and repeatedly, and round and round, with scarce-concealed jealousy, that the loving heart must be pure also, and must give undivided allegiance, and think of "no-other," and must keep close to him, must bear him in mind constantly; the individual soul must never again lose its recovered memory of, and touch with, the Universal Oversoul. God is Love: God is insatiate of Love; the Oneness of God, the all-pervading, all-uniting, and Immortal Self, is the very nature, the very essence of the sense, the feel, of Love;[97] hence Love is Immortal. Alas, that Hate—Satan, Manyness, the sense of separateness, Divisiveness[98]–should be correspondingly and necessarily immortal also![99] "He who loveth much, much shall surely be forgiven him."

> अपि चेत्सुदुराचारो भजते मामनन्यभाक् ।
> साधुरेव स मंतव्यः सम्यग्व्यवसितो हि सः ॥ *Gita*, ix, 30.

"He who loveth *Me-not-another*, even though he be wrong in conduct now, he will righten soon; his heart is set aright." "The family wherein faces are glad, and eyes full of affection, and hearts rejoice in each other– God, who is Love, necessaily rejoices there greatly."

---

[97] अभेदबुद्धिः

[98] भेदबुद्धिः Writers on politics too, even in the West, are beginning to recognise the vital significance and incalculable value of this sense of non-separateness of "self-and-others," and consequent possibility of "co-operation," "co-adaptation," etc., in social or "group"-organisation, and the recognition is naturally affecting their whole thought and phraseology; see, *e. g.*, Miss M. P. Folletts' *The New State* (1926).

[99] The *Mahatma Letters*, p. 127.

वदनानि प्रसन्नानि स्निग्धान्यक्षीणि यत्र च ।
प्रीयंते बाधवा यत्र तत्रैव रमते हरि : ।।

Buddha's Sermon of the Greatest Blessedness, the "Maha-mangala Sutta," says the same. The atmospheres of love and of hate are more positive facts, and more life-nourishing and life-destroying, respectively, than balmy breezes and simoom-blasts. The element of loving devotion in religion draws people together into congregations and new nations, states, civilisations; but the forces of lust, hate, and greed very soon open wide again "the triple gateway into hell," and cause disintegrations. Witness the fate of all faiths; schisms begin even in the lifetimes of the founders, and certainly afterwards. The One and the Many are both operating perpetually and simultaneously. Emphasis on the general, the common, aspect, interest, belief, ideal, purpose, makes for expansion and growth; on the peculiar, the specific, the distinctive, separative, exclusive, makes for diminution and decay.[100] The seeing of similarity in diversity is science, the Science of the Finite; the seeing of unity in diversity is Philosophy, the Science of the Infinite; the active functioning of such Unity amidst Diversity, in human life, is *varna-vyavastha*, social organisation, is good co-operative economics, civics, politics, and civilisation generally. How to keep the Many (parts or particular or singular ones) subordi-

---

[100] सर्वदा सर्वभावानां सामान्यं वृद्धिकारणम् ।
ह्रासहेतुर्विशेषश्च प्रवृत्तिरुभयस्य तु ।।
सामान्यमेकत्वकरं विशेषस्तु पृथक्त्वकृत् ।
तुल्यार्थता हि सामान्यं विशेषस्तु विपर्ययः ।।

*Charaka Samhita* (on Medicine), I, i.

nated to and co-ordinated in the Whole Universal One, the sectarian to and in the humanitarian, the exclusive *bhakti* for *a* one to the inclusive *bhakti* for *the* One which is the All, is the great problem. As the *Bhagavata* says:

> सर्वभूतेषु यः पश्येद्भगवद्भावमात्मनः ।
> भूतानि भगवत्यात्मन्यसौ भागवतोत्तमः ॥
> ईश्वरे तदधीनेषु बालिशेषु द्विषत्सु च ।
> प्रेममैत्रीकृपोपेक्षा यः करोति स मध्यमः ॥
> अर्चायामेव हरये पूजा यः श्रद्धयेहते ।
> न तद्भक्तेषु चान्येषु स भक्तः प्राकृतः स्मृतः ॥ XI, ii.

"He who sees the glorious Lordship of the Self manifest equally in all beings, and all beings in the Lord Self (Bhagavan Atma), he is the best and highest Bhagavata, the true *bhakta* and servant of the Lord. He who adores the Lord, loves his devotees, pities the immature, and keeps aloof from sinners and haters, he is the *bhakta* of the lower, the middling, quality. He who is always offering worship to some particular form or image, and has no affection for fellow-creatures, he is a *bhakta* of bad quality."

> वदन्ति तत्तत्त्वविदः तत्त्वं यज्ज्ञानमद्वयं ।
> ब्रह्मेति परमात्मेति भगवानिति शब्द्यते ॥ I. ii.

"Bhagavan, the Lord of all, Param-Atma, the Supreme Universal Self, Brahman, the Infinite, are all names for that essential Principle of Consciousness which the sages declare is One-without-Another, One-without-a-second [I-another (This)-Not]."[101]

Bhakti at this level fuses and becomes one with Jnana and Karma; Right Thought, Right Desire, Right Action

[101] *Tawhid-la-tashrik,* in Sufi phrase.

become inseparable aspects of, and almost simultaneous with one another.

But for earlier stages, the three yogas are distinguished from on another. The third, seventh, and twelfth chapters of the *Gita* are respectively entitled Karma-Yoga, Jnana-Yoga and Bhakti-Yoga. All the other chapters have also names ending with the word *Yoga;* but they may all be classified under these three,[102] and regarded as expositions of details. In the *Bhagavata*, Krishna says to Uddhava:

योगास्त्रयो मया प्रोक्ताः नृणां श्रेयोविधित्सया ।
ज्ञानं कर्म च भक्तिश्च नोपायोऽन्योऽस्ति कुत्रचित् ॥
निर्विण्णानां ज्ञानयोगो न्यासिनामिह कर्मसु ।
तेष्वनिर्विण्णचित्तानां कर्मयोगस्तु कामिनाम् ॥
यदृच्छया मत्कथादौ जातश्रद्धस्तु यः पुमान् ।
न निर्विण्णो नातिसक्तो भक्तियोगोऽस्य सिद्धिदः ॥

XI, xx, 6-8.

"I have declared three ways for the good of human beings, the paths of knowledge, of devotion, of action. The first is for those who are surfeited with the world, tired of restless movement, wishful to understand its final how and why, and to pay off and have done, to perform only that action which is *due*, is *duty*, which would be of the nature of repayment of old debts[103], not of the contracting of new ones, so as to free them from old bonds and not bind them with new ones. The last is for those who are full of eager appetites and restless ambitions for the things of the world. The second is

---

[102] The three expressions occur in the text also in the third, fifth, thirteenth, and sixteenth chapters. See the Word-Index of the *Gita*.

[103] नैष्कर्म्य.

for those who are neither tired wholly, nor yet eagerly ambitious, and who have come somehow to hear of Me and are anxious to know more about Me."[104]

In the twelfth chapter of the *Gita*, Krishna mentions to Arjuna a number of alternatives, which may be understood as broadly corresponding to these. "Perform this *yoga;* if you cannot do it, then do this else; if not even this, then follow this other *yoga.*" Each is suited to one state and stage of the journeying soul.

The word *yoga* occurs very frequently in the *Gita;* almost as much so as *buddhi* and *jnana.* It comes from the Samskrt root *yuj, yunj,* the same as the Latin *jugare, jungere,* to yoke, to join. It principally means joining. It has dozens of meanings now; *e.g.,* arming for battle, a device, a medical recipe, a meeting of persons, conjunction of planets, attention and contemplation, etc.[105] The last, *viz.,*concentrated attention, meditation, has come to be its special and technical meaning. But all these senses have developed out of, and are allied together by, the primary and essential significance which runs through them all, obviouly, *viz.,*that of joining one thing to another. The joining of the body, mind, heart, soul, to, the engaging of it in, some object, some method of acting, some way of feeling, some mode of thinking, for the achieving of happiness—this is the idea

---

[104] Broad correspondences are, in Buddhism. *Samma-sambodhi* and Maha-yana. Pratyeka-bodhi or Majjhima-yana or Eka-yana. and Sravaka-bodhi or Hina-yana : in Jainism. *Jnana, Samyak-darshana, Charitrya*: in Islamic Sufism. Haqiqat. Tariqat, and Shariyat : in Christianity. Gnosticism. Mysticism, Ceremonialism and Good Works. The psychological basis of all these is, of course, the triple function of individualised consciousness. *viz..* cognition-desire-action.

[105] योग: सन्नहनोपायध्यानसंगतियुक्तिषु. *Amara-kosha.*

running through the three *yogas* of *karma*, *bhakti*, *jnana*. The joining of the individual soul with the Universal Soul, to the extent of, in the sense of, realising the "non-separateness," the identity, of the two, *i.e.*, of all—this is the culmination of *yoga*.[106] With reference to this condition, *yoga* is defined in the *Gita* as

यं लब्ध्वा चापरं लाभं मन्यते नाऽधिकं ततः ।
यस्मिन् स्थितो न दुःखेन गुरुणाऽपि विचाल्यते ।
तं विद्याद् दुःखसंयोगवियोगं योगसंज्ञितम् ।। vi, 22, 23.

"Having gained which condition, the soul regards no other gain as equal in value; firmly fixed in which, the soul is not shaken from its inner serenity by any the severest storms of life, the worst strokes of fortune, the most painful ills; that is the true *yoga;* that whereby the individual is united with the Universal and disunited from all painful limitations and separations."

Distinguishing between the cognitional (*chit*)and actional (*sat*) or practical aspects of the above, which may be regarded as the "emotional" (*i.e.*, *ananda* and *shanta*) aspect, this same *yoga* is defined in the *Gita* elsewhere as

समत्वं योग उच्यते ।
योगः कर्मसु कौशलम् । ii, 48, 50.

"Equanimity, sameness of inner mood. equal-mindedness in occasions of joy and of sorrow, success and failure, gain and loss (*i.e.*, *samadarshita*)—this is *yoga*. Skill, propriety, correctness, rectitude, in action, unerring performance of whatever is the right thing to do, in every situation—this is *yoga*."

[106] *Gita*. vi. 15 : the words *nirvana*, *moksha*, *nisshreyas* occur in the *Gita* for this state.

These three may be regarded as the three aspects of *yoga* accomplished, completed, in the metaphysical sense, dealing with the *attitude* of the soul to life and the world, on all planes whatever. Various psycho-physical practices, ethical disciplines, spiritual exercises, constitute *yoga*-methods. technically, in the sense of the *Yoga-darshana*, the Yoga system of Philosophy and Practical or Applied Psychology. They are *yoga* in course of accomplishment, with reference to the attainment of the metaphysical attitude generally, as well as the achieving of particular *siddhis* specially.[107]

The three *yogas*, of *karma*, *bhakti*, and *jnana*, are also known as *marga-s*, paths, ways. As described in the quotation from the *Bhagavata*, they find their appropriate use in succession, one after another in the journey of the *jiva* through its cyclic life. First comes the restless bodily movement of the early years; the young live in action, in play. Then comes restraint and selection of activity, and definite direction of it by predominant desire; the middle-aged live in ambitions. Finally, we have decrease of physical movement and increase of thought; the old live in memory. The *regulation* of each of these ways of nature, for the purpose of facilitating the soul's progress, converts it into a *yoga*, a systematic method. The three may be said to have, each, a narrower, lower, earlier, form and sense, and a broader, higher, later one. The rationalism, devotionalism (or mysticism), and practicalism of the narrower kind, in the earlier stage, are capable of being more clearly distinguished, or even to some extent separated, from each other, and are followed respectively by persons of different temperaments (*i.e.*, "men of knowledge," "men of feelings-emotion-desire" and "men of action"), who when

[107]*Gita*, VI, 3.

animated by greater zeal than discretion, as they generally are in the early stages, tend to fall out, with one another, even violently; witness the streams of blood, running across the pages of history, shed in sectarian factions and religious wars. In their higher form they seem to coalesce, as above indicated, though still distinguishable, and the travellers thereon co-operate for the well-being of the world—so it seems from such accounts of the Spiritual Hierarchies as are available in the literatures of the various religions.[108]

In the narrower sense, *karma-yoga* may mean the fixed routine of daily domestic and social duties, and also the round of small rites and ceremonies, *karma kanda*, which occupies the time of those who can neither sit still nor do anything better and more useful, and the excess of which Krishna condemns so

---

[108] See notes at pp. 133-135,142, *supra*. Compare the many grades and kinds of Mukta-s, Rshi-s, Deva-s, Manu-s, Kumara-s, etc., in the Veda-scheme ; the Arhat-s, Asekha-s, Nirvani-s, Para-nirvani-s, Bodhi-sattva-s, Buddha-s, etc., in Buddhism ; Siddha-s, Tirthankara-s, etc., in Jainism; Angels, Archangels, Sons of God, Powers, Principalities, Thrones, etc., in Christianity ; Nabi-s, Auliya-s, Abdal-s, Autad-s, Qutb-s, Farishta-s, etc., in Islamic Sufism. "The Wali-s ( Auliya ), from the highest to the lowest, are arranged in a graduated hierarchy, with the Qutab (the Pole) at their head, forming a saintly board of administration by which the invisible Government of the world is carried on. . . . The Autads are four saints whose rank is little inferior to that of the Qutb himself"; Nicholson, *Studies in Islamic Mysticism*, pp. 78-79. Others mention three Autads below the Qutb, and seven Abdals below them, each in charge of a continent ; others speak of forty Abdals : *Ibid.*, pp. 194, 195, and Glossary appended to Khaja Khan's *Studies in Tasawwuf*. Theosophical literature speaks of One Lord of the World (the earth) named Sanat-Kumara (the Eternal Virgin), three Kumaras or Pratyeka-Buddha-s under him, then a Manu, a Buddha, a Maha-Chohan, then seven Chohan-s, then some fifty or sixty Masters.

strongly[109]. In the larger sense, it might mean the complete Code of Life.[110] including plane after plane and cycle after cycle in its scope, as the *mukta jiva*, the "liberated soul," progresses in renunciation and world-service, and utilises for such service the greater *jnana*, or rather *vijnana*, of Nature's subtler forces, "occult science," *Gupta-vidya*, *Veda-rahasya*, which, the traditions say, is imparted to such soul by its custodians in the Spiritual Hierarchy of which that soul has now become a member, or is discovered by it through its own *yoga* efforts. This "occult practical science" may be said to constitute the science of *Power* as distinguished from Metaphysic, the Science of *Peace*. The one belongs to the region, or, rather aspect, of Change; the other to that of Changelessness. The "sacraments" and "magic ritual" performed by such *siddha jiva-s*, "accomplished souls," *dikshita-s*,[111] initiates, would be just as different from the ordinary ritualist's manoeuvrings, and in the same sense, as the physical scientist's applications of his science for the performance of great works, from the juggler's tricks and imitations. Indeed, "occult science" seems to be "science," nothing more or less, but, so far, "hidden" from common knowledge, as steam and electricity and wireless and aviation were utterly "occult science," a century ago.[112]

---

109 "They want something new. A ritual to amuse them"; The *Mahatma Letters*, p. 266 : see also pp. 111 and 399.

110 कर्मयोगश्च वैदिकः । *Manu*.

111 The word seems to be used in this sense in *The Mahatma Letters*, pp. 97, 281.

112 In the note appended to the section on Ritualism *vs.* Wisdom, above, the "secret" meaning of the Veda has been referred to. The *Rg-veda* itself refers to this hidden meaning :

So *Jnana-Yoga*, in the lower sense, would mean intellectual studies of all kinds, and, more especially, philosophical enquiry. In the larger and deeper sense, it would seem to mean realisation of the Utlimate Truths of Atma-vidya, clear and certain knowledge of the basic Laws of Nature, and an ever

---

उतत्वः पश्यन्न ददर्श वाचं उतत्वः शृण्वन्न शृणोप्येनाम् ।
उतोत्वस्मै तन्वं विसस्रे जायेव पत्य उशती मुवासा : ॥ VIII, ii. 23.

"The ordinary person seeing sees not, and hearing hears not. The Sacred Word unveils itself and shows its hidden meaning only to the deserving, as a loving bride displays her beauty to her loving husband."

Manu's injunction, that the Veda should be studied with its *rahasya* or secret meaning, has been already referred to. He further says :

आद्यं यत् त्र्यक्षरं ब्रह्म त्रयी यस्मिन् प्रतिष्ठिता ।
स गुह्योऽन्यस्त्रिवृद्वेदो यस्तं वेद स वेदवित् ॥ XI. 265.

"The primal three-lettered Brahman, on which the Triad is founded—that is another, and secret, threefold Veda ; he who knows *that*, *he* knows the Veda." This verse seems to refer to the AUM, the Pranava, which has a science of its own, which science (as the *Pranava-Vada* indicates tantalisingly) amounts veritably to omni-science. The Gita-verses viii, 13, and xvii, 23, 24, regarding AUM, should also be considered in this connection. Some old commentators incline to think that this *guhya* or *rashasya* or secret meaning of the Vedas is nothing else than the *Jnana* embodied in the Upanishats, Atma-Vidya, the Science of the Infinite Self, the realisation of the individual self's identity with which brings peace. But others seem to think that, though this Jnana is, no doubt, all-important, more so than any other knowledge or experience, physical or superphysical, yet that this *rahasya* is not only this science of peace, but also includes, besides, a science of power, hidden away in the formulae of the Karma-kanda (the *Samhita* and *Brahmana* portions of the Vedas), and also of the Jnana-kanda (the Upanishat portions) to some extent ; that the Veda has not only an *adhyatmika* or metaphysical (Subjective, Spiritual) aspect and meaning, but also *adhi-daivika* and *adhi-bhautika* meanings (Objective and Material, physical and superphysical, relating to subtle forces), which constitute " occult " science, psycho-physical *Vijnana*,

expanding grasp of "occult" science, that aspect of Yoga in the technical sense which is specially concerned with *siddhi-s*, extra-ordinary "accomplishments" or powers, "extensions of faculty," etc.

So *Bhakti-Yoga*, in the narrower sense, begins with the fixing of faith in, and worship, in the hope of some reward, of,

---

"special knowledge" of particular energies working in the region of the finite, *i.e.*, of Changeful Matter of various planes, as distinguished from *Jnana* in the sense of the science of the Infinite Spirit (*Gita*, ix, 1). That AUM, as the Primal Sound, the Word that was with God and was God, has, as such Sound (apart from the meanings assigned to the three letters which constitute its written symbol in Samskrt), a supreme super-physical potency—is something which also belongs to that Science of Power. This Primal Sound, the chief of all *mantra-s*, might be called the sound-"continuum" or the "general sensation" of sound (in the language of modern psychologists), of which all special or particular sounds are modifications. It would be the first originator of vibrations and the first manifest expression of vital Emotion and Intention, Cosmic Ideation, Buddhi.

That all this occult science of power, however great and extensive and intensive its functioning, still falls within the *Apara Vidya* or Lower Knowledge, and belongs to the region of the changeful and the finite, the region of Avidya, is made clear by these verses of the *Matsya Purana* :

अथर्वऋग्यजुःसाम्नां वेदेष्विह पृथक् पृथक् ।
ऋषीणां तप्यतां तेषां तपः परमदुश्चरम् ॥
मंत्राः प्रादुर्भवंत्यादौ पूर्वमन्वंतरस्य ह ।
असंतोषाद् भयाद् दुःखान् मोहाच् छोकाच् च पंचधा ॥ ch. 145.

"The Rshis, undergoing the most difficult ascetic penances, made their re-discoveries of the *mantras* (magic-chants, ideas, symbols and formulae intelligible to and usable by the initiated and expert, like those of chemistry and mathematics) under the impulsion and profound emotional stress of Discontentment, Fear, Pain, Compassion, and Sorrow." Compare the five stages, in the *Yogadarshana*, of Avidya, Asmita, Raga, Dvesha, Abhinivesha. Manu also says : काम्यो हि वेदाधिगमः; "(the Karma-kanda of) the Veda has its root in Desire-Kama" which covers all the

all sorts of natural and artificial objects, ranging from the pettiest stocks, stones, idols, amulets, and fetishes to the grandest suns and stars. The *faith* of the worshipper, which is a form of the Will-force of the Great Self present in him also, though he be unconscious of the great fact, makes such worship too effective, even in those cases where the object of the worship is not a real living entity, capable of direct response.

यो यो यां यां तनुं भक्तः श्रद्धयार्चितुमर्हति ।
तस्य तस्याचलां श्रद्धां तामेव विदधाम्यहम् ॥
स तया श्रद्धया युक्तस्तस्याराधानमीहते ।
लभते च ततः कामान् मयैव विहितान् हितान् ॥

*Gita*, VII,21, 22.

ये यथा मां प्रपद्यंते तांस्तथैव भजाम्यहम्।
मम वर्त्मानुवर्त्तंते मनुष्याः पार्थ सर्वशः ॥ IV,11·
येऽप्यन्यदेवताभक्ता यजंते श्रद्धयान्विताः ।
तेऽपि मामेव कौंतेय यजंत्यविधिपूर्वकम् ॥ IX. 23.
त्रिविधा भवति श्रद्धा देहिनां सा स्वभावजा ।
सात्त्विकी राजसी चैव तामसी चेति तां शृणु ॥ XVII, 2, 4.
यजंते सात्त्विका देवान् यक्षरक्षांसि राजसाः ।
प्रेतान् भूतगणांश्चान्ये यजंते तामसा जनाः ॥

---

five motives of the *Matsya-Purana*). The inarticulate but intensely significant cries of birds, animals, children, and adult human beings, expressive of fear, anger, pain, pleasure, joy, sorrow, sympathy, antipathy, discontentment, satisfaction, coaxing, soothing, encouragement, support, request, etc., etc., are all modifications of the AUM, and may be connected with corresponding sounds and forces in Nature.

The Sufis also distinguish between *Ilm-i-sina* and *Ilm-i-safina*, "heart-knowledge" and "page-knowledge". In one aspect, this corresponds to *Para* and *Apara*, or Higher and Lower, Knowledge; in another to *Aparoksha* and *Paroksha*, Direct Realisation or first-hand experience and Indirect second-hand knowledge. See *The Secret Doctrine*, I, 39, 68.

यांति देवव्रता देवान् पितॄन् यांति पितृव्रताः ।

भूतानि यांति भूतेज्याः यांति मद्याजिनोऽपि माम् ॥ IX, 25.

"Whichever form anyone makes object of adoration, the I satisfies his desires through that same form. All forms and all paths and all worshippers are Mine, all belong to the I ultimately. The I therefore meets every worshipper on his own road, in his own way. Even they who worship other gods with faith and aspiration, they also worship Me, though in irregular ways; for indeed all living things are striving, albeit unconsciously, the vast majority of them, to find the I, to attain Self-consciousness, to find the Universal I, the Greatest God of all. There are three kinds of faithful aspiration,[113] *sattvika, rajasa,* and *tamasa*. Persons of the *sattvika* quality worship the *devas* (angels, beneficent gods); those of the *rajasa*, the *yaksha-s* and the *raksha-s* (spirits of a lower quality); those of the *tamasa*, *preta-s* and *bhuta-s* (ghosts and evil spirits).[114] Worshippers of other forms go to those respectively; worshippers of Me come to Me, *i.e.*, seekers of the Universal Self attain that Self." In the larger sense, *Bhakti-yoga* is, primarily, as said in the quotation made above from the *Bhagavata* as regards the three grades or qualities of *bhaktas*, deliberate, conscious, immersion in the infinite feeling of identity with all life, with the whole universe, the whole World-process; and secondarily, it is immense and intense compassion for the younger and weaker, outwelling affection for the compeers, unswerving loyalty and deepest

---

[113] श्रद्धा, श्रत् सत्यं दधाति यया सा, श्रदिति सत्यनामसु पठितव्यम् ।

Yaska, *Nirukta*.

" That mood of mind whereby the soul clings to truth, clings to some thing as being the truth, holds it fast as the truth"; *shrat*, truth, *dha*, to hold.

[114] Such endeavour, by human beings, to establish relations with *devas* and *upa-devas*, spirits of high and low degree, good and evil quality, *i. e.*, the deva-loka generally, on the one hand, is as natural as with the animal

reverence for the Elders, all helping and holding on to each other, and travelling, side by side, behind, before, and after one another, but all together, on the Endless Path of everlasting Lila, Unceasing World Drama. Such *Bhakti-yoga* constitutes the link between the higher *Jnana-Yoga* and *Karma-Yoga*. Desire is the nexus between cognition and action.

As the old books say:

भक्तिः परेशानुभवो विरक्तिरन्यत्र चैष त्रिक एककालः ।
प्रपद्यमानस्य यथाऽश्नतः स्युः तुष्टिः पुष्टिः क्षुदपायोऽनुघासम् ॥
इत्यच्युतांघ्रिं भजतोऽनुवृत्त्या भक्तिर्विरक्तिर्भगवत्प्रबोधः ।
भवंति वै भागवतस्य राजंस्ततः परां शांतिमुपैति साक्षात् ॥

*Bhagavata*, XI, iii, 42, 43.

एवं तु पंडितैर्ज्ञात्वा सर्वभूतमयं हरिं ।
क्रियते सर्वभूतेषु भक्तिरव्यभिचारिणी ॥ *Vishnu Purana*.

मय्येव मन आधत्स्व मयि बुद्धिं निवेशय।
निवसिष्यसि मय्येव अत ऊर्ध्वं न संशयः ॥
मन्मना भव मद्भक्तो मद्याजी मां नमस्कुरु ।
अहं त्वां सर्वपापेभ्यो मोक्षयिष्यामि मा शुचः ॥
यो मां पश्यति सर्वत्र सर्वं च मयि पश्यति ।
तस्याहं न प्रणश्यामि स च मे न प्रणश्यति ॥ *Gita*.
यस्तु सर्वाणि भूतानि आत्मन्येवानुपश्यति ।
सर्वभूतेषु चात्मानं ततो न विजुगुप्सते ॥ *Isha*.

---

and vegetable kingdoms, on the other. It is all due to the fact of "symbiosis," mutual dependence and co-operation between all the departments of Nature, only another aspect of *abheda*, the non-separate continuity and organic unity of the whole of the World-process (*Gita* iii, 10,11). "The Universal Mind, having created the several orders or kingdoms of beings, by and with sacrifice, impressed upon them the law that they would all prosper by sacrifice, self-sacrifice, of each for the sake of the others."

एवं यः सर्वभूतेषु पश्यत्यात्मानमात्मना ।
स सर्वतामेत्य ब्रह्माभ्येति परं पदम् ।। *Manu.*

"Consciousness of the Universality of the Self, Love universal, renunciant self-denying service of All–these three arise simultaneously with the taking of spiritual noursihment; as health, strength, and freedom from hunger, with that of physical food. They who see Hari[115] in all beings, they thenceforth give *bhakti*-love to all beings. He who puts his mind, his heart, in(the)Me, he dwells in (the) Me[116] ever; put thy heart in Me, put thy mind in Me, and (the) I will deliver thee from all sorrows.[117] He who beholds all beings in the Self, and the Self in all beings, he can never feel lost, he can never hate anyone again, he attains the final peace that comes from the realisation that self-and-others are all One-Self."[118]

---

[115]हरति दुःखानि इति हरिः, "He who removes all sorrows."

[116]"Walking with God", "Abiding with God", "Dwelling in the Lord,' " Being filled with the Holy Spirit," are similar Biblical expressions.

[117]Compare the Biblical sentence : "Come unto (the) Me, all ye that are weary and heavy-laden, and (the) I will give ye rest."

[118]Without the clue of some such simple metaphysical principles as are attempted to be indicated above, Krishna's teachings in the *Gita* would probably remain to many students, as they did for long to the present writer, an un-co-ordinated and confusing heap of more or less disjointed, separate, even inconsistent, "mystical" and mystifying ideas. And those principles are to be found all over the world in the utterances of the Self-seers. For instance, Omar Khayyam :

> "Where All is One, there is no room for sorrow,
> Nor for this gaudy Myth of you-and-me ;
> These what we call yestreen—to-day—to-morrow
> Merge in the Moment of Eternity."

Which seems to be a fair rendering of the Upanishat-verse :

तत्र को मोहः कः शोकः एकत्वमनुपश्यतः । and of another :
भूतं भवद् भविष्यच्च सर्वं मय्येव विद्यते ।

Love Universal—this seems to be the significance of *Bhakti* at its best and highest. A measureless ocean of Parental Compassion seems to flow perpetually throughout the World-process from the senior to the junior jivas, and a corresponding ocean of Filial Reverence flows unceasingly from the juniors to the seniors. This seems to be the life-blood of the Universe-Organism, which nourishes, cleanses, integrates and renovates it incessantly, and provides the working material of the beneficent spiritual hierarchies. It is noteworthy that the highest heavens ( the Buddhic plane) of most of the living religions are depicted as filled with angels, *farishta-s*, *awliya-s*, saints, *rshis*, *mukta-s*, etc., all perpetually engaged in the one function of *prayer and adoration* of the Supreme. As said before, the *Gayatri*-mantra is but such archetypal prayer-willing. In the elemental, primal, form, life is but such continual circulation of Energy. Personal Prayer and Response mean only the additon of personal consciousness to Nature's supra-or sub-conscious operations. To open the nostrils and the lungs to the morning breeze is the best physical prayer to

---

though it is not reported whether Khayyam had or had not access to the Upanishats. in original or translation.

The pair of technical words, in Sufism, for " feeling of non-separateness " or *abheda-buddhi* and " sense of separateness " or *bheda-buddhi* seems to be *ittisal* and *infisal*. The footnote at p. 56 speaks of the " disappearance of the desire for liberation ". The disappearance of all personal separative selfish desire *is* liberation. The dawn of the *abheda-buddhi*, of the sense of Union, *ittisal* or *wisal* with the Beloved Supreme Self, is liberation from and annihilation of the sense of separateness, limitedness, smallness, mortality, fear, doubt, selfishness, etc., is fulfilment of, and therefore liberation from, all desire. The Buddha's annihilation of self, is obviously annihilation of selfishness, the feel of the small self.

the breeze. To bathe in the winter sunlight is the best physical prayer to the Sun. So to open out one's individual *prana-buddhi* for the inflow of the vital energy and inspirations of the Universal Prana-Buddhi, for the well-being of all, is the best prayer to the Supreme, and the most potent functioning, it would seem, of the Spiritual Hierarchies. All other particular or special beneficent functions may be said to become resolved into, and, again, to take their rise out of, this one general function, even as all bodily activities may be said to be the transformations of the primary activity of breathing.

Unfortunately, but inevitably, there are also corresponding oceans and counter-currents of the maleficent and disintegrating emotions, as toxic secretions in the living organism.[119] And these opposed and exhaustless streams are intermingling everywhere. Material sheaths, bodies, worlds, planes of matter, are only settings or basins for their surging torrents. And souls are bathing, diving and emerging, in all, turn by turn.[120] As the *Dhyana-bindu Upanishat* pictures the process, "the jiva is always moving round and round the petals of the heart-chakra, which is like an open lotus, and each petal is a reservoir of one kind of feeling."

---

[119]See *The Science of the Emotions.*

[120]Cf. *Yoga-bhashya,* i. 12,

चित्तनदी नामोभयतो वाहिनी, वहति कल्याणाय, वहति च पापाय

"The stream of conscious mind flows in two opposite directions ; it leads to good, and it leads to evil also."

And Maulana Rum, *Masnawi* :

Bahar-i-talkh o bahr-i-shirin ham-enan :
Darmiyan shan barzakh-e-la-yubghiyan.

"The oceans of sweetness and of bitterness surge side by side : between them is the region of peace."

Peace from this ceaseless turmoil can be found only by passing from the radii to the centre, the Self, and holding fast to It, tying oneself to It with the strong bond of Prayer (as above explained), and thereafter consciously trying one's best to guide other younger jivas, through the reservoirs of the various kinds and degrees of purer and purer *bhakti*-love, to the same Central Self.[121]

Similes derived from the human family, of husband and wife, of parent and child, of brother and sister, of elders, youngers, and compeers, are not to be despised. They cannot be improved upon. They have not been improved upon, but have been diligently used, by the philosophies and ethics which constitute the common heart of all the great religions, in trying to explain the essential fundamental principles of Life and the World-process. As repeatedly said, in all these philosophies, the infinitesimal is as the infinite, the microcosm as the macrocosm, the atom as the solar system, the *kshudra-virat* as the *maha-virat*, man as God: nay man *is* God; for our quest is completed, our heart attains rest, only when we have found God *in* man, in one-self, in my-Self. As said before, all relations are exhausted as between Purusha and Prakrti, I and This; so the spiritual affections and relations of parent and child, and brother and sister, as well as the psycho-physical love-passion of man and woman, all are included in and spring out of the relation of husband and wife. Human love and divine love are not different in kind, but only aspects of

---

[121]सर्वाजीवे सर्वसंस्थे बृहंते तस्मिन् हंसो भ्राम्यते ब्रह्मचक्रे ।
पृथगात्मानं प्रेरितारं च मत्वा जुष्टस्ततस्तेनामृतत्वमेति ॥

*Shvetashvatara Upanishat*, i, 6.

one another. The "Maha-mangala Sutta" of the Buddha provides high testimony, if any be needed.[122]

---

[122]The Sufi-s speak of the correspondences between *ishq-i-mazazi*, "imitational" or "counterfeit" human love, and *ishq-i-haqiqi*, true divine love.

The law of analogy, same-sightedness, *sama-darshita* has been amply recognised by them.

Muhaqqiq hamin binad andar abil
Ke dar khub-ruyan-i Chin o Chagil.

*I.e.*, The wise see in the camel's frame
The same laws manifest
As in the beauteous Chinese dame
Or Chagil's belle, the best.

Which is almost like a translation of the *Gita*-vese, v. 18. Another Sufi couplet says :

Gar tajalli khas khwahi surat-e-insan bi bin ;
Zat-i-Haq ra ashkara andarun khandan bi bin.

*I.e.*, Wouldst thou behold God wholly manifest ?
Look at thy brother's kindly face awhile.
Wouldst see Divinity at its sweet best ?
Then call forth on that brother's face a smile.

*Maha-bharata*, Shanti-parva, Ch. 305, says :

गुह्यं ब्रह्म तदिदं वो ब्रवीमि न मानुष्यात्श्रेष्ठतरं हि किंचित् ।

"There is nothing higher than Man : I speak this to you as the last word of secret wisdom". And the *Bhagavata* (XI, ix, 28) explains :

सृष्ट्वा पुराणि विविधान्यजयाऽऽत्मशक्त्या वृक्षान् सरीसृपपशून् खग-
दंशमत्स्यान् । तैस्तैरतुष्टहृदयो मनुजं विधाय ब्रह्मावबोधधिषणं मुदमाप देवः ॥

"God made vesture after vesture for Himself—vegetable forms, insects, fishes, reptiles, birds, mammals. But His heart was not satisfied. Then He created and donned the human shape. In this body He was able to know Himself, the Infinite. Then was He glad." The Bible and the Quran also declare that "the human body is the living temple of God."

The subject of eugenics and physical culture has been referred to at p. 71, *supra*. It should be assiduously borne in mind, in this connection, that psychical, ethical, *spiritual* culture—by fostering and strengthening

That even after the attainment of *jnana*, *bhakti* is natural and indispensable, is indicated by Krishna in the *Gita* (XII,

---

the *spiritual affections*, as distinguished from *physical sex-passion*, with the help of ennobling and elevating religious exercises of *bhakti* directed towards *high ideals*—is far, far, more necessary than mere *physical* culture. While the strength and shape of the muscles of the body may be temporarily improved by the latter, beauty of *mind* and *face*, and lasting health, and virility of the finer kinds, will not be secured without the former. The pampering of the sensuous-passion-aspect of sex, of *kama*-lust instead of *bhakti*-love, the belittling and despising of male and female virginity before marriage, the ignoring and flouting of the psycho-spiritual strength o will and refinement of mind and lasting freshness of emotion that is gained by such virgin *brahma-charya* (enjoined by Manu), before entering the household life,—of all which there is much indication in western literature today (*e.g.*, in Mr. Lindsey's *The Revolt of Modern Youth* and *Companionate Marriage*, published in 1927 and 1928, in which useful and mischievous ideas are greatly mixed up),—has already led to the war-*madness* of 1914-1918, as will be seen when the deep underlying psychological causes of the Great War are studied (—it was the same in the case of the Mahabharata War—), and will do so again, in worse way, and will complete the ruin of civilisation, if not checked in time. Hate is the twin-brother of Lust, and simply cannot be separated from it. " No pains, no gains " is sound metaphysical axiom. To think that Nature can be cheated and defeated by artificial devices, and that it is possible to filch sensual pleasurs from her without paying heavy price, is to imagine that the problems and theorems of geometry can be solved even after flouting all its definitions, postulates, and axioms. War there must be ; but human beings have a choice : they can carry it on *within* themselves, between their higher nature and their lower nature ; or *without*, between each other's physical bodies, with murder and devastation on a vast scale. Pain there must be : but human beings have a choice : they can infiict and suffer it, each on and in his own lower nature : or on one another's bodies and minds. By the former choice they rise higher in civilisation of soul and body. By the latter, they fall lower. Indulgence of the selfish and coarse passions, feeds, by its effluvia, corresponding evil spirits, *yaksha*-s, *raksha*-s, disease-bacilli, and strengthens and attracts them, and they help to hasten the downward course. Fostering the higher nature, similarly provides ethereal

3,4,5).[123] "They who seek and find and devote themselves to the Changeless, Unwaning, Ineffable, Unmanifest, All-pervading, Unimaginable, Formless, Immovable, Rock-seated, Certain-most, Axial: they who approach It with restraint of the senses, with equal-mindedness towards all things everywhere: they also come to Me (as Personal Ishwara of the particular world-system to which they belong) and, through Me and with Me, to loving service of all their fellow-beings. But their way, the way of the Abstract, is the more difficult. The Bodi-less is not easy to grasp, for the em-bodied. (Yet It has to be comprehended, some day, sooner or later)." The classical illustration of this *Vedanta-siddhanta*, this metaphysical and psychological principle, is supplied, as usual, by *Purana-Itihasa*, in the story of how the *Bhagavata Purana* came to be composed by Vyasa. This story is given in the *Bhagavata* itself.

The great Rshi, who had labored all his long life single-mindedly for the *education* and enlightenment of the people, had collected the "*One* primeval Veda"[124] and rearranged and

---

nourishment for the higher *deva-s*. evokes their help and promotes healthful secretions and nerve-forces. Modern western science has come to recognise the fact of "symbiosis." "co-operation." "mutual influence," "mutual dependence," between the vegetable and the animal kingdoms. It will, by and by, if permitted by the menacing armies of Lust and Hate and Greed to carry on its work, come to recognise similar symbiosis between these and the *deva* and other kingdoms (angels, *farishta-s*, *malayak-s*, etc., good and bad).

[123]See the foot-note to these verses in Annie Besant and Bhagavan Das's *Bhagawad-Gita*.

[124]एक एव पुरा वेदः प्रणवः सर्ववाङ्मयः ।
एको नारायणो देवः एकोऽग्निर्वर्ण एव च ॥
वेदमेकं स बहुधा कुरुते हितकाम्यया ।
वेदानां व्यसनाद्व्यासश्चतुर्वेकस्य हि स्मृतः ॥

edited and published it as the now current *four* Vedas, had compiled many *Purana-s* and the *Maha-bharata*, had framed the *Brahmasutra-s*, had taught them unremittingly to whole universityful of students (five of whom carried on his work after him)—the great Rshi sat, unhappy, sad at heart, dry in soul, after the Great War, on the bank of the Saraswati in the Himalaya mountains, where his *tapo-vana* and *guru-kula*, "ascetic forest" and "university," were located. Narada came to him. "Why so sad?" "You know all hearts; tell me the reason yourself, and the remedy too." "You have cultivated and spread *Jnana* only and not *bhakti*. Sing high and far and sweet the glories of the Lord, open the flood-gates of *bhakti*, personal as well as impersonal and universal.[125] Let that life-giving stream flow forth over the land, fertilising all minds, refreshing and revivifying all hearts. Then your parched and thirsting soul will also be moistened with the waters of tenderness, and will rejoice and bathe in *ananda*." And Vyasa did so. Even Kevali-s, Pratyeka-buddhas, "Soli taries," are only comparatively so. They too have to work in co-operation with others, in some way or another, so long as they wear any *kaya*, any body, at all. They too have to be *bhakta-s* of their Elders, lovers of their equals, tend-ers of their youngers. "Nothing in the world is single; all things, by a law divine, in one another's being mingle";[126] Mine-Thine both are Mine. And genuine sincere *bhakti* for Krishna necessarily means *bhakti* for his teachings also; the following of them in the setting of the *Sanatana Dharma*, the Permanent Laws of human nature, and of the *loka-sangraha*, the social organisation, based thereon: the unfailing preformance, by

[125]The Persian Sufi poets have made the combination splendidly.

[126]Shelley.

all, of general human duties common to all persons, and by each, of his special duty in his particular position in the social organism.

## NOTE

A convenient doctrine is strongly urged by one class of profess-ors of *bhakti*, that in the present age of Kali it is enough to chant litanies, shout "Haribol," "Kyrie eleison," repeat the name, "Allah, Allah," "Rama, Rama," "Krishna, Krishna," to be absolved from all sins. The old books severely condemn such blatant, brazen, hypocrisy.

स्वधर्मकर्मविमुखाः कृष्णकृष्णेति राविणः ।
ते हरेर्द्वेषिणो मूढाः धर्मार्थं जन्म यद्धरेः ॥

"They who deliberately neglect their *duties* and simply shout Krishna, Krishna, unctuously and hypocritically, they are not votaries but enemies of Krishna ; since He incarnated on the earth for no other purpose than to re-establish the shaken Dharma, and teach human beings to discharge their lawful *duties* to one another." Jesus censured those who were too fond of crying "Lord, Lord," and of saying their prayers in the synagogues and the streets to display their piety. And the Prophet Muhammad had occasion to advise a new and therefore over-zealous convert, who was saying his *namaz*-prayer much too loudly : "Friend ! Allah is not deaf ; He will hear you even better if you pray silently, but sincerely."

The sect which is specially devoted, in India, today, to Krishna-worship (as distinguished from worship of Vishnu, Narayana, Rama, Chaitanya or Gauranga, etc., the last-mentioned being also believed by his followers to be an incarnation of Krishna, in Bengal, in the fifteenth century A.D.) is that of Vallabha Acharya, born towards the end of the fifteenth centry A.D., about which time there was a great uprush of *bhakti*, all over India, marked by the birth and preachings of many saints, in north, south, east and west, and the output of much devotional literature, poetical song and hymn as well as reasoned disquisition and biography, in Samskrt as well as Hindi, Marathi, Bengali, Gujarati, etc. The philosophy of Vallabha's "way" gives it the name of the *Pushti-marga* (to distinguish it from the ordinary three *margas*). The word means, "the way of the ulness of life," "of life well-nourished by the divine grace of Krishna." It has developed its own minor type of culture, way of living and speaking, peculiarities of language, social conventions, forms of salutation, etc. Every religion, and even sect, as said before (p. 14 *supra*), impresses its mark on the people's life in all its departments. For example, "At the opening of the modern period, interest centred around the Protestant Reformation. Beginning as a religious movement, it became increasingly political in nature, and the doctrines of its leaders, especially of Calvin, influenced the theory of the state." (Gettell, *Political Science*, p. 77 ; pub. 1910). But this sect has not troubled itself with political affairs and theories of the state. The philosophy of the fulness of life would be all right, if it included not only grace and joy, but strenuous struggle against evil, as Krishna's life pre-eminently did. But the sect ignores altogether that aspect of the great life. Krishna, the super-hero, the matchless warrior, the unrivalled statesman, the expeller of the Rakshasas, the breaker of the militarist oppressors of the people, the maker and consolidator of Yudhishthira's empire, the creator of the vast and beautiful capital city on the sea-coast, the experimenter with republicanism, the Teacher of the *Gita*—is unknown to the ordinary follower and votary of the sect. The sect's conception, in practice, of "the fulness of life" is limited to the dwelling on and enacting of the scenes and doings of Krishna's childhood and adolescence, of his flirtations and dances with the dairy-maids, and the enjoyments of tongue and sex—which elemental appetites somehow manage to become the chief objects of worship, in one disguise or another, in most of the sects of all religions. Some graces and refinements of conversational language and social manners (inclining towards euphemism, euphuism, effeminacy, and unctuosity) and some love and patronage of fine art may be regrded as virtues to its credit, as a set-off.

An instructive piece of local history seems worth recording here. Popular memory, in and around Mathura and Vrndavana (spelt as Muttra and Bindraban nowadays), the chief centres of Krishna-worship to-day (though the headquarters of the sect are at Shri-Nath-dwara in Udaipur territory), reports that about two centuries ago, a *go-swami* (the "official desigantion" of the *guru-s* of the sect) there grew much too fond of enacting Krishna's milk-maid *lila-s* with his women-disciples. The then *raja* (king) of those tracts happened to be a true protector of his people and not a despoiler and devourer of them as so many have been. He called up the "spiritual preceptor". "Why do you do this ?" "I have

10

the spirit of Krishna in me." "Then perform the Govardhana-*lila* also." (The legend will be remembered that Krishna lifted up with his left hand the Govardhana hill, and put all the cattle of the country round about under neath it, to protect them from an exceptionally violent thunderstorm of hail and lightning created by Indra's spite. The "preceptor" wished to take leave because of urgent business. The *raja* ordered his soldiers to "help" him to perform the *lila* and prove the spirit of Krishna in him. They stood him up, and put upon him a two-ton stone slab, to represent the Govardhana hill. The *guru* never performed any *lila-s* again.

A theory has been started by some members of the Theosophical Society that the biography of Krishna as currently accepted in India is made up of two lives ; that there were two Krishnas, one at the time of the Mahabharata war, the warrior and statesman and teacher of the *Gita*, and another much later, in or near Vranda-vana, who was the devotion-inspirer, the beloved of votaries. This may be true, or may be an error. Of course, nothing is impossible. Jesus Christ is said, by some, to have been born anything like 4 or 5 to 105 B.C. ; the Vikrama era, of which this is the year 1986, to have been "thrown backwards" by quite four hundred years, reason not known ; Shakespeare to be the same as Bacon; and so on. But the earlier and the later incidents of Krishna's life, as currently accepted, on the basis of the *Mahabharata*, *Bhagavata*, etc., show no such hopeless incompatibility as would by itself give *prima facie* ground or justification for such a theory. (See *The Secret Doctrine*, I, Introduction xliii). The question does not seem to possess any special practical importance either, though much general intellectual interest, as a matter of accuracy in history. Possibly not only one but many attractive, charming, devotion-inspiring personalities have appeared in India, from time to time (like Gauranga-Chaitanya, the "Fair-limbed, the Vital, the Intelligent." mentioned above), in the course of the many centuries that have elapsed since the Krishna of the Mahabharata days. Possibly portions of the super-physical sheaths, the *sukshma-sharira*, etc., of the glorious vesture worn by the original Krishna, were preserved, and were "inherited" and used by some of these later manifestations, as the robes of state and crown jewels and weapons and throne made for and used by a great sovereign may be used by his successors. Sections xliii and xliv of *The Secret Doctrine*, Vol. III, on "The Mystery of Buddha" and "The Reincarnations of Buddha," mention such utilisation of "astral remains" and "principles"; and the *Mahabharata* and the *Bhagavata* and other Puranas mention many other similar "mystical" facts, for which we have good analogies in familiar daily life. in accord with the luminous law of *sama-darshita*. Thus, the cases of Arjuna and Karna, whose bodies were compounded out of several previous " personae ", have been already mentioned in the text. So Krishna too was an " incarnation " of the Rshi Narayana, as well as a " hair from the head of Aditya-Narayana ". His contemporary Vyasa was also a partial manifestation of Narayana. Yudhishthira was a previous Indra, and also the son of Dharma; and Vidura was an incarnation of Yama, and quitted his physical body by standing up against a tree and " looking fixedly into Yudhishthira's eyes, till he (Vidura) *passed into* Yudhishthira," Yama being Dharmaraja. " While Yama was on earth, incarnate in Vidura, the god Aryama officiated for him as ruler of the Pitr-world." And so on. A few simple metaphysical principles, the laws of analogy, of continuous unity in diversity, of universal commingling, of individuality-in-universality and *vice versa*, help us to understand, a little.

## Duty, Organisation, Synthesis;

## The Rational Practicalism Of The Gita

As integral part or indispensable corollary of this final teaching of philosophy and ethics, Atma-vidya, as the rational practice which is the natural, legitimate, and proper outcome of this spiritual rationalism and practical devotion, we have the doctrine of लोकसंग्रह, *loka-sangraha*, in the setting of which *loka-sangraha*, human duties arise. *Loka-sangraha* means world-synthesis, world-col-lec-tion, world-binding-together, world-organisation, the organisation of the Human Race, the assignment of each individual to his proper place in society and in the state, the division of labor, of remuneration, of means of livelihood, and of the rewards and prizes of life, in accordance with the natural division of temperaments and functions, as ascertained by psycho-physio-logy or Adhyatma-shastra.

लोकसंग्रहमेवापि संपश्यन् कर्त्तुमर्हसि ।
कुर्याद्विद्वांस्तथाऽसक्तश्चिकीर्षुर्लोकसंग्रहम् ॥ *Gita.*
यल्लोकहितमत्यन्तं तत्सत्यमिति नः श्रुतम् । *Mbh.* Shanti.

"The wise man should act so that he may promote social organisation and co-operation, and not violate its principles." "We have heard this also that that is the Truth, the Good, the Right, which is most useful, most beneficial, most happiness-bringing, to Humanity." In this verse we have the essence of utilitarianism, the whole of whatever element of truth there is in the doctrine of "the greatest happiness of the greatest number." It should be particularly noted in this reference, that Krishna, in the *Gita*, bases the "caste" system, not on "heredity," but on "spontaneous variation."

चातुर्वर्ण्यं मया सृष्टं गुणकर्मविभागशः ।
कर्माणि प्रविभक्तानि स्वभावप्रभवैर्गुणैः ॥

"*Swa-bhava, i.e., Prakrti,* the *nature* of the Self, has three ***guna-s;*** their respective predominance makes the respective 'twice-born' class-castes, the man of thought (*sattva*), the man of action (*rajas*), the man of (acquisitive, clinging) desire (*tamas*)' with the undifferentiated as a fourth; and the duties of the four are divided accordingly." The *Bhagavata* and other Puranas mention *many* cases of change of caste of whole families and clans, and not only the solitary. and as if exceptional, case of Vishvamittra. Thus the *Kshattriya* king Rshabha-deva had a hundred sons, of whom "eighty-one became *Brahmanas*. Prshadhra, a *Kshattriya* prince, became a *Shudra*. the descendants of the *Kshattriya* Dhrshta became *Brahmanas* under the clan name of Agni-veshyayana-s. Nabhaga, the son of the *Kshattriya* king Dishta, became a *Vaishya*".

एकाशीतिर् . . . ब्राह्मणा बभूवु. । (Sk. V. ch. 3.)
पृषध्रः शूद्रतां गतः ।
धृष्टाद् . . . ब्रह्मकुलं जातमाग्निवेश्यायनं नृप ।
नाभागो दिष्टपुत्रोऽन्यो कर्मणा वैश्यता गतः ।। (IX, ii.)

And again:

शर्यातिर्मानवो राजा ब्रह्मिष्ठः स बभूव ह ।
यो वा अंगिरसां सत्रे द्वितीयमह ऊचिवान् ।। (IX, iii.)
दुरितक्षयो महावीर्यात् तस्य त्रय्यारुणिः कविः ।
पुष्करारुणिरित्यत्र ये ब्राह्मणगतिं गताः ।। (IX. xxi.)
गर्गाच्छिनिस्ततो गार्ग्यः क्षत्राद् ब्रह्म ह्यवर्त्तत ।
मुद्गलात् ब्रह्म निर्वृत्त गोत्रं मौद्गल्यसंज्ञितम् ।। (IX, xxi·)

"Sharyati, the son of Manu, became a high *Brahmana*, and officiated as priest in the sacrifice performed by the Angirasa-s. The *Kshattriyas* Durita-kshaya, Trayyaruni, and Pushkararuni became *Brahmanas*.[127] From the *Kshatriya* Garga was born Shini, and from Shini was born Gargya who became a *Brahmana* (and a famous astrologer); and from the *Kshattriya* Mudgala was descended the clan of the Maudgalya *Brahmanas*." And so forth.

When the social organisation is justly planned, co-operation becomes natural, every one knows his duty clearly, and finds no difficulty in performing it. It is the business of the great man, the leader, the ruler, the man in power and authority, to secure this rational social organisation first of all. Then all good things else will add themselves. For only by such systematic and scientific organisation may

[127] See, now, that excellent work, C. V. Vaidya's *History of Medieval India* (in three volumes) generally, and Vol. II, Book v, ch. 2, on "Caste and Social Condition," specially.

the greatest happiness of the greatest number be achieved. It is the essence and the foundation of all good politics and civics; the *forms* of government and local administration are comparatively inessential, superstructural.

Not exclusivenss but synthesis, not "this *only*" but "this *also*," is the key-note of the whole of the best Sanatana Dharma culture—whatever the character of its present degenerate form may be. Give every thing, every idea, every custom, every person, its or his or her *proper* time and place and circumstance, and you develop the best that there is in it or him or her. Also, lay more stress on *duty* than on *right*—the *duty* of every *class* of individuals as well as of every individual. This is an essential characteristic of the ancient Sanatana Dharma. The modern tendency is to lay more stress on the rights than on the duties of the individual, on the contrary. Right and Duty are the obverse and the reverse aspects of the same thing, Dharma or Law. Dharma (*dhr*, to hold and bind together), Law (*legere*, to bind, that helps to hold human beings together in society), binds together a duty and a corresponding right, and it thereby binds together human beings also, in the bonds of such mutual rights-and-duties. Insistence on either will secure the other also, generally. But there is a difference. Childern may be taught either by fear or by love. They may be led and attracted forwards, or pushed from behind. Is there any doubt as to which is the better way? Everybody insistently claiming and taking his rights from everybody else—this is one way of maintaining society. Every one eagerly giving to every one else the latter's dues, eagerly performing his own duties–this is another way of doing the same thing. Which is the better? Generally, in history, it is only when the so-called "higher", "upper," or stronger classes, in positions of power and authority, forget their own duties and the rights of others too much, that the others begin to reciprocate, and frictions and class-wars begin. For peaceful progress, it is absolutely necessary that each class and each individual should think more of its and his duties than rights. This does not mean that fear and punishment and pain and claim of rights, etc., ought to or can be wholly abolished from human life and education, any more than they can be from Nature. To think so would be going to the opposite and equal error of the other extreme; and Dharma eschews all extremes. Fear and pain, etc., also have their own appropriate subordinate place.

The four psycho-physical types of man, the man of thought, the man of action, the man of desire, the undifferentiated and unskilled worker; the four corresponding vocational classes in each complete communiy which are the four natural estates of every realm, and, when made mutually helpful and affectionate, by equitable distribution of necessaries and luxuries, make it civilised and prosperous; the four corresponding sets of duties-and-rights: the four kinds of special rewards, honor, power, wealth, and play; the four main kinds of livelihood; the four main interests or ends of life; the four corresponding stages in each lifetime—these are the main features of the synthetic scheme of division of the social labor and of its rewards, division of work and play, which had been disturbed by the excessive preponderance of the militarist elements in his day, and which Krishna sought to restore. A proper, psycho-physically scientific, organisation of society is the only foundation for all sound economics, civics, and politics;

for it will reconcile, by giving to each its due, the claims of individualism amd socialism, which are both indefeasibly present in all human *society* made up of *individuals;* and the Varnashrama Dharma *does* this. But this is not the place to expound how it does this work, in detail.[128] Yet, as further illustration of the comprehensive, all-including, all-embracing, nature of Sanatana Dharma, we may note such facts as its synthesis (*not* mutual exclusion), of the four "colors" of human beings *in one community,* with necessary scientific safeguards against degeneration of specific characteristics by too indiscriminate marrriages, its recognition of eight kinds of marriages, twelve kinds of sons, four kinds of funerals, etc., each with its proper circumstance. Even in the matter of such an apparently slight but really important affair as salutation, we find many forms illustrated by Krishna. When he returns from Indra-prastha (Delhi) to Dwaraka, he greets his various kinsfolk, elders, equals, youngers, dependents, in various ways.

प्रह्वाभिवादनाश्लेषकरस्पर्शस्मितेक्षणैः । *Bhagavata.*

On another occasion,

ततोऽवतीर्य गोविंदो रथात्स च युधिष्ठिरः ।
भीमो गांडीवधन्वा च यमौ सात्यकिरेव च ।
ऋषीनभ्यर्चयामासुः करानुद्यम्य दक्षिणान् ॥ *Maha-bharata.*

---

[128]The whole subject has been treated of at length, in the writer's *The Science of Social Organisation*, in *The Science of Politics, in the Light of Brahma-Vidya* (which appeared as a series of articles in *The Theosophist*, August, 1919, to March, 1920, but has not yet been published separately in book-form); and in two pamphlets, *Social Reconstruction*, and *Social Reconstruction with special reference to Indian Problems*; also now in a work in Hindi, under the title of *Samanvaya* ( synthesis or Reconciliation), published by the Bharata Bhandara, Benares.

"By low obeisance, by spoken salutation (*svagatam*, 'welcome,' *su-prabhatam*, 'good morning'), by embrace, by handshake, by tender caress, by smile, by glance, by lifting the right hand, etc." Such are instances of लोकसंग्रह, which Krishna teaches by precept and by example.

## NOTE

The *principles* of Manu's Scheme of Social Organisation, repeated very briefly by Krishna in the *Gita*, and detailed by Bhishma in the Shanti-parva of the *Maha-bharata*, if *properly* interpreted and applied in modern conditions, can solve all human problems and reconcile Individualism and Socialism, Capitalism and Communism, by pointing out the rational middle course between their irrational and erroneous extremes, and by obviating the *psychological* difficulties which are being ignored by all the belligerents in the present chaotic war and welter of *isms*. Psychological difficulties can be overcome only by psychological devices. Human affairs can be administered successfully only with the help of the laws and facts of human nature. Hence Manu applies the principles of psychology and philosophy in organising human society. Western thinkers are beginning to realise that the difficulties, in the way of the success of each and all of the many and very various schemes covered by the word Socialism, are *psychological* (Gettell, in his *Political Science*, and Bertrand Russell in his *Roads to Freedom*), while it is also generally recognised that the excesses of so-called Individualism must be checked. And they are gradually approaching those psychological and metaphysical principles which alone can provide the remedy for the prevalent disease. Thus, Viscount Haldane's Introduction to Miss Follett's *The New State* (1926), and much of Part I of the work, may be regarded as a commentary on Manu's dictum :

न ह्यनध्यात्मवित् कश्चित् क्रियाफलमुपाश्नुते ।

" No one who ignores the principles of philosophy and psychology can bring any human activities to successful issue." But this commentary is naturally perplexed as yet, and suffers from the bias of a lop-sided Philosophy of Change, unsubordinated to and unbalanced and uncompleted by the as yet unrecognised Philosophy of the Changeless, without which

Atma-vidya is *vidya* without the Atma. Still it is all very promising, and it may be hoped that the balance will be found before very long.

Some quotations may be made, with running comments, to bring out the contacts with ancient Indian thought. "As an individual I am the undivided one, in the group-I, I am again the undivided one, as the state-I, I am the undivided one—I am always and for ever the undivided one, mounting from height to height, always mounting" (p. 319, quoted at p. xii of Haldane's Introduction). This is a recogniton, and an application to politics, of the law of individualities within individualities, *jivatmas* within *sutratmas*, and these within higher and larger *sutratmas*, souls within oversouls of higher and higher degrees, species within genera, but without clear recognition that each always reflects the Unity of the Changeless Universal Self. (See *The Science of Peace*). "No Government will be successful which does not rest on the individual on his better side, and . . . this better side is to be reached neither by sending more people to the poll, nor by sending them more frequently" (*Ibid.* p. xitv). "The more intimate and spiritual is the enterprise, the more does the true honor and reward restrict itself to what lives 'in those pure eyes and perfect witness of all-judging love" (Prof. Bosanquet quoted at p. xvii, *Ibid*)." Representative Government has failed." "*Group organisation* must be the new method in politics" .... "But who is the individual...we are to find within the group ? Certainly not the particularist individual. ... The fallacy of self-and-others fades away and there is only self-in-and-through-others, only others so firmly rooted in the self and so fruitfully growing there that sundering is impossible." . . . "The enthusiasts of democracy to-day are those who have caught sight of a great spiritual unity which is supported by the most vital trend in philosophical thought and by the latest biologists and social psychologists." "Neighbourhood and occupational groups, either independently or one through the other, must both find representation in the state" (pp. 5, 6, 8, 156, 321). It is to be hoped that these ideas, now "confessedly embryonic" (p. 320), will develop strongly in the West, and attain completion of growth andclear definition of good shape. Manu's scheme, and the philosophy it is based upon, embody these ideas in their well-defined form ; but their clear light has become clouded and their significance forgotten, in the course of ages—in order, perhaps, that they may be re-learnt, perhaps with greater fulness and richness of content, in communion with the new western nations, by new groups of souls, taking birth in India, in the long course of the World-Drama. It is only necessary to mention the old Samskrt words —" Swa-rajya " (legislation and rule by the higher Self of the people, their wisest, best, most spiritual select and elect, see pp. 118-9, *supra*);[129] the " brahmana-type " of person, self-denying, ascetic, spiritual, philanthropic, strongly realising the unity of his self with all selves, content with appreciation and honor, not desirous of mundane material wealth) ; *varna-vyavastha* (group organisation); *bheda-buddhi* (the fallacy of self-and-others, the *maya* of many selves separate from and exclusive of each other, the illusion of the sense of separateness between the particularist individualist me and other particulrist individuals—which, though an illusion, is yet a fact to be recknoned with); *abheda-buddhi* (the sense of comm-unity with others, *i.e.*, of the non-separate unity of all, the recognition of the organic unity and continuity of Nature)—to indicate the approaches between the ancient and this latest modern thought. This unity of all selves is indeed patent, since obviously the same psychic mind-stuff, the same ideas and emotions and volitions, and the same physical material, solid, liquid, gaseous, is constantly circulating through all illusion-separated individual forms, as the ocean-water through all billows, waves, whirlpools, bubbles. A general and instinctive-intuitive recognition of this is proved by the very word " member," meaning limb of body as well as component of committee, association, community, society, race, etc. *Bani Adam aza-i yak digar and,* say the Sufis ; " the children of Adam are all limbs and organs of one another." " The main occupational or functional groups are as head, arms, trunk, and legs, in the organism of the body politic," says Manu, following in the wake of the Vedas.

ब्राह्मणोऽस्य मुखमासीद् बाहू राजन्यः कृतः ।
ऊरू तदस्य यद् वैश्यः पद्भ्यां शूद्रोऽजायत ॥ *Purusha Sukta.*

## RAJA-DHARMA

The great teaching on the subject of *loka-sangraha* which Krishna gave in detail, not directly, himself, but by the mouth of Bhishma, which is the completion of the

---

[129] See, in this connection, the Introduction, by the present writer, and the Appendix ("Outline Scheme of Swa-raj " by C. R. Das and Bhagavan Das), to *The Coming Renaissance*, by P. M. L. Varma (The Indian Press, Allahabad).

teaching of the *Gita*, and is its application to the administration of the People's life—this teaching is unfortunately too much neglected in India, nowadays. At the beginning of the Mahabharata war comes the *Gita* which nerves Arjuna for the struggle. At its end appropriately comes the teaching of Bhishma to Yudhishthira, given and received by Krishna's express wish, on the all-important subject of the true Science and Art of Politics, दंडनीति, राजधर्म, राजशास्त्र, spiritualised by Atmavidya—by means of which alone can the work of the reconstruction of a People shattered by a terrible internecine war, be sucessfully carried out, and Krishna's work as an avatara be completed. By means only of a spiritualised "politics-civics-economics," can a just and righteous great man, leader and ruler, make Satya-yuga out of Kali-yuga.

दंडनीत्यां यदा राजा सम्यक् कार्त्स्न्येन वर्त्तते ।
तदा कृतयुगं नाम कालः श्रेष्ठः प्रवर्त्तते ।।
दंडनीतिः स्वधर्मेषु चातुर्वर्ण्यं नियच्छति ।
लोकस्य सीमंतकरी मर्यादा लोकपावनी ।
सम्यङ्नीता दंडनीतिर्यथा माता यथा पिता ।।
मज्जेत् त्रयी दंडनीतौ हतायां सर्वे धर्माः प्रक्षयेयुर्विरुद्धाः ।
सर्वे धर्माश्चाश्रमाणां हताः स्युः क्षात्रे नष्टे राजधर्मे पुराणे ।।
सर्वे धर्मा राजधर्मेषु दृष्टाः सर्वा दीक्षा राजधर्मेषु चोक्ताः ।
सर्वा विद्या राजधर्मेषु युक्ताः सर्वे लोका राजधर्मे प्रविष्टाः ।।

*Maha-bharata*, Shanti-parva.

"When the ruling element conducts the affairs of the people in accordance wih a just and sound and far-sighted and all-comprehensive (and not patchwork, haphazard and opportunist) policy—then society is properly organised, with its four vocational classes duly articulated together, and each observing its duties in accordance with law and order. Such High Science of Policy, well and righteously administered, is even as father and as mother unto the people. All sciences subserve it; all laws and all high secrets are to be found in it; all the well-being of all humanity depends upon it. If it fail and fall from just and righteous wisdom, all social order would sink into confusion, and all science and art would disappear into chaos."

Such is the teaching outlined by Krishna himself directly, and given in greater detail by the mouth of Bhishma; for Bhishma, too, was a superman, and second only to Krishna.

### The Passing Of Bhishma

The circumstances in which this teaching was delivered are indicative of the quality of the giver. In his last great battle with Arjuna, the aged "grandfather" (openly desiring victory for the righteous Pandava brothers, though bound by various reasons to fight on the side of their unrighteous cousins, the Kaurava brothers), smiling benignly, scolding Arjuna for not shooting his arrows more strongly, trying to provoke him to do so by his own hits, wishing to be overthrown by no lesser warrior than his favorite pupil and grandson Arjuna—Bhishma, the rightful heir to the throne of Hastinapur, who, in his splendid youth gave up his right to it, in an instant, and took oath to remain unmarried and pure all his life, in order to enable his widowed father to marry again, the woman whom he had chosen, but who would not marry him until the throne was assured to her progeny, not only as against claim by Bhishma but also as against possible contest by any son of his—Bhishma was ultimately pierced with so many arrows, under the angry commands of Krishna, by the very grieved and very unwilling Arjuna, that he fell fainting from his chariot to the ground, towards the close of day. But yet his body could not touch the ground, because of the thickly projecting shafts—as quills from a porcupine, is the simile used in the epic. The battle halted for a moment. The warring cousins, and the other great leaders, ran up. They wished to remove him; he commanded otherwise. They brought the most skilful surgeons; he declined their service. Death came to free him from his tortured body; no, Death must wait till the Sun turned to the north, for a *Yogi* like Bhishma, master of life and death—he was one of the eight great "gods" who make the order of the Vasu-s in the divine hierarchy, in the ancient Indian Pantheon, come to earth to play a part in the terrene portion of the world-drama, in consequence of a doom laid upon him by the sage Vasishtha (also a name for the Sun) for some passing manifestation of desire with respect to that same eternal "Earth-cow" (mentioned before)— a great soul like Bhishma's must not leave the fleshly body till that auspicious season for voyaging back to the Sun came round. Also, the body, though tortured, had even more useful work to do yet than it had ever done before. And so, barricades were made, and watchers placed; and Arjuna made peculiar mechanical arrangements for drops of water to fall into his grandfather's mouth, as he lay on that bed of arrows feeling no other want than that of the drinking water, which he would accept from no other hands than those of Arjuna. And the battle raged for eight more days all around him, and flickered out. Then Bhishma called, in his soul, to Krishna. Krishna heard that superphysical cry as he was conversing with the desolate Yudhishthira, in the distant camp, trying to console the inconsolable king, demented by the awful slaughter of his nearest and dearest, kith and kin and relatives and friends, and the devastation of the whole country. Then, in order that himself may be near to his votary, that Yudhishthira may learn wisdom, and that Bhishma's greatness and glory may also thereby receive its crown and be known to all the future generations, Krishna led Yudhishthira to the feet of the dying warrior, to be consoled, by learning anew, from his mouth, the principles of *Raja-Dharma*, the Royal Science, the Science of Kings, the King of Sciences, which teaches how human affairs should be administered for the good of all human beings, and how all other sciences should be directed and utilised for that good. And a great company of venerable *rshis* and *munis*, sages and saints, as well as soldiers and householders, gathered round that wonderful god-man, and, in reverent silence—Yudhishthira questioning from time to time—heard the words of precious all-synthesising wisdom, issuing from his lips. And because rulers, put in a position of authority over men, are so apt to become intoxicated with power, and to think that that power comes to them by some birthright, some divine right of their own, for their own enjoyment, and does not come from the Divinity, the *Brahma*, the Cosmic Ideation, the Universal Mind, the *Mahat-Buddhi*, which is as much in the People as in them; because they so often forget that whatever power they have is entrusted to them by the explicit or the tacit Will of the People, for the People's Welfaring—because of this danger, Bhishma impressed upon Yudhishthira the duty of loving as well as fearing the People too, as Yudhishthira's other "grandfather" Vyasa also impressed upon him on other occasions.

खनीनेत्रस्तु विक्रांतो जित्वा राज्यमकंटकम् ।
नाशकद्रक्षितु राज्यं नान्वरज्यंत तं प्रजाः ॥
तमपास्य च तद्राज्ये तस्य पुत्रं सुवर्चसम् ।
अभ्यषिचंत राजेंद्र मुदिता ह्यभवंस्ततः ॥
स पितुर्विक्रियां दृष्ट्वा राज्यान्निरसनं च तत् ।
नियतो वर्त्तयामास प्रजाहितचिकीर्षया ॥
ब्रह्मण्यः सत्यवादी च शुचिः शमदमान्वितः ।
प्रजास्तं चान्वरज्यंत धर्मनित्यं मनस्विनम् ॥

*Maha-bharata*, Ashva-medha-parva, ch. 4.

"Khani-netra, the son of Vivimsha, failed in his duty of protecting and promoting the welfare of the People, and the People liked him not, and arose against him, and cast him out, and appointed his son Suvarcha in his place.[130] And Suvarcha, beholding the fate of his father, took lesson from his vices and their consequences, and did his duty, and strove assiduously for the well-being of the People, and was full of all manly and kingly virtues, and the People rejoiced in him and with him, and loved him and helped him in all ways."

Such wise things Bhishma taught to Yudhishthira until the fifty-eighth day after his fall from the war-chariot.

At the dawning of that day, they all gathered round him as usual, and Yudhishthira addressed him: "Open

---

[130] *Manu*. Kautilya's *Artha-shastra*, and the Puranas and Itihasas mention many other instances of the punishment of bad rulers, by the people through the Rshis.

your eyes, dear grandfather and true King of the whole land! The blind king Dhrita-rashtra and Yudhishthira salute you. The holy sages are present also, with the sacred fires of your house. And the lord of us all, Krishna-Vasudeva, is here too. Instruct us in our duties." Then Bhishma slowly opened his eyes and saw them all, and moving a little, and raising his arm, he spoke, in his own old voice of the rain-laden clouds. "I am glad thou hast come, and all these others. The million-rayed Lord of Heaven, who makes the day, has now turned to the north.[131] Eight and fifty nights have I lain here over these sharp-pointed shafts, and the time has passed slow as a hundred years.

अष्टपंचाशतं रात्र्यः शयानस्य च मे गताः ।
शरेषु निशिताग्रेषु यथा वर्षशतं तथा ।।

I must pass on now to other worlds. Follow Dharma and be to the King Dhrita-rashtra as a son, as I know thou wilt be." Then he turned to Krishna, and, with many words of glad and reverent praise, asked consent: "Give me permission, Krishna, to cast off this body of flesh; with your consent alone, may I pass on to higher worlds."

---

[131] A Purana -verse says :

यमस्य दूताश्च तथैव पार्षदा नारायणस्याथ गणाः शिवस्य ।
सूर्यस्य रश्मीनवलम्ब्य सर्वे जीवान् नियच्छन् ( न्तः ) विचरंति सर्वदा ।।

"The messengers of Yama, the councillors and ambassadors of Narayana, the host-leaders of Shiva, flash with the speed of thought, on the pathways formed by the rays of the Sun, all over the realms of space, to adjust the affairs of living beings."

स मां त्वमनुजानीहि कृष्ण मोक्ष्ये कलेवरम् ।
त्वयाऽहं समनुज्ञातो गच्छेयं परमां गतिम् ॥

And Krishna said: "I give thee permission; go unto the Vasu-s, thou stainless soul, whose will the Lord of Death himself obeys." Then Bhishma once again to all: "Follow the Truth always; strive for it ever, in thought and word and deed, O Children of the Bharata—Motherland! Seek for and find the Infinite and Eternal within yourself, be self-denying, be compassionate. That is the supreme Dharma of all Dharmas. Where Krishna, the Universal Self, which attracts all to Itself [132] is, there Dharma ever is; and where Dharma is, there always is unfailing triumph."

सत्येषु यतितव्यं वः सत्यं हि परमं बलम् ।
आनृशंस्यपरैर्भाव्यं सदैव नियतात्मभिः ॥
ब्रह्मण्यैर्धर्मशीलैश्च तपोनित्यैश्च भारताः ।
यतः कृष्णस्ततो धर्मो यतो धर्मस्ततो जयः ॥

And he closed his eyes again, and steadily gathered, by concentration, all his vital forces in the head, and thence passed out as a great light which rose into the heavens and disappeared in an instant. And even to this day, because Bhishma had no son of his own body to offer him water, therefore all Indians who offer the prescribed ceremonial

---

[132] कर्षति सर्वान् यः, अथवा कृष्यंते स्वयमेव सर्वे जीवाः यं प्रति, स कृष्णः, "That which draws all to Itself, or, to whom all living things and beings are attracted of themselves, is Krishna," from *krsh*, to attract; and such is the One Universal Self Al(l)-one.

oblations to the departed, offer water unto him, not that the great soul of Bhishma the Vasu-god needs such water, but that the souls of those who offer it may be lifted up by their mood of grateful reverence, and be brought into psycho-spiritual touch with him, and be strengthened and sanctified by the high ideal he represents.

वैयाघ्रपाद्यगोत्राय सांकृतिप्रवराय च ।
अपुत्राय ददाम्येतत्सलिलं भीष्मवर्मणे ॥

So passed Bhishma, the paragon of blameless knights, the chevalier *sans peur et sans reproche*, the type of perfect kshattriya-hood, after having, as the crowning work of his life, re-uttered to Yudhishthira, as a legacy and trust for all future generations, for the helping of mankind, the essential principles of a just and equitable division of the rights and duties of individuals as well as classes.

If any statesmen of to-day, when conditions of militarism and luxuriousness and oppression of the weak are somewhat similar to those of Krishna's day, really want a reconstruction and a stable organisation of society, they would not altogether waste their time if they consulted those teachings of Raja-Dharma for ideas and principles, instead of spending all their energy in making economical and political experiments with lop-sided mechanical devices which rely on external compulsion and which take no account of human psychology or Atma-vidya, with its self-working devices of inner implusion, and therefore lead only to vicious circles of farcical and tragical failures. If the life of Krishna is duly studied and the principles taught by him and his devotee Bhishma are followed, then may much success in achieving human happiness be attained.

## Conclusion

The story of Krishna is truly as instructive as it is sweet.

"May He inspire our minds with wisdom, He who is the Teacher of the Teachers; for, without that wisdom, we ever blindly take up courses of action which we fondly hope will bring us joy, but which always plunge us into only deeper miseries. No higher motive-force of work is there for us, than to dwell upon Thy greatness, Lord! Do for us Thyself, whatever may be good for us, as wise and strong parents do for their unknowing and all-helpless children. The illustrious men of fame, the generous benefactors of their fellow-mortals, the men of open-handed charity, the strong-willed and self-denying ascetics of many vows and vigils, the seers of the Vedic hymns, the discoverers of great policies for guiding the affairs of men—none such attain success in their respective lines of work without their seeking Thy help in silent prayer within the chamber of the heart. To think Thee, to sing Thee, to salute Thee, to worship Thee, to behold Thee—this cleanses hearts of sins at once. We bow before Thee, therefore, in loving adoration. Who can ever be surfeited with hearing of Thy works! Their infinite story distils nectar and ambrosia with every word into the minds of those that know its blissful taste. The Servants of the Lord who tell that deathless story, the Servants of the Lord who listen to it—they learn full soon the Oneness of the form-ful Finites with the Form-less Infinite, which is the One Sole Secondless and Otherless Unconscious Consciousness, I-Not-Another, enthroned in every living heart, in every atom-point, including all Space and all Time and all Motion within Itself, which the wise call by the names of Brahman and Paramatman and Bhagavan."

चरित पुनीत सुनत हरि के नित नित चित तृप्ति न जोहैं ।
पद पद मे जाके निसरत रस रसिकन के मन मोहैं ।।
वयं तु न वितृप्याम उत्तमश्लोकविक्रमे ।
यच्छृण्वतां रसज्ञानां स्वादु स्वादु पदे पदे ।।
जनोऽबुधोऽयं निजकर्मबंधनः
मुखेच्छया कर्म समीहतेऽसुखम् ।
यत्सेवया तां विधुनोत्यसन्मति
धियं स नोऽव्यात् परमो गुरोर्गुरुः ।।
भवद्गुणानुस्मरणादृते सतां
निमित्तमन्यद् भगवन्न विद्यते ।
पिता चरेद् बालहितं यथा स्वयं
तथा त्वमेवार्हसि नः समीहितुम् ।।
यशस्विनो दानपरास्तपस्विनो मनस्विनो मंत्रदृशस्सुमंगलाः ।
क्षेमं न विदंति विना यदर्हणं तस्मै सुभद्रश्रवसे नमो नमः ।।
यद्वंदनं यत्स्मरणं यदर्हणं यत्कीर्त्तन यच्छ्रवणं यदीक्षणं ।
जनस्य सद्यो विधुनोति कल्मषं तस्मै सुभद्रश्रवसे नमो नमः ।।
वदन्ति तत्तत्त्वविदः तत्त्वं यज्ज्ञानमद्वयम् ।
ब्रह्मेति परमात्मेति भगवानिति शब्द्यते ।।
जेइ दास भगवान कहैं यह जेइ दास भगवान सुनैं ।
तेइ चीन्हि भगवान गुनन कौ निर्गुन सगुन अभेद गुनैं ।।

ॐ

सर्वस्तरतु दुर्गाणि सर्वो भद्राणि पश्यतु ।
सर्वः सद्बुद्धिमाप्नोतु सर्वः सर्वत्र नंदतु ।।

ॐ

## NOTE

### KRISHNA'S TEACHING OF NIS-TRAI-GUNYA

Two ways of thinking are current on the subject of the connection between Vedanta and Dharma-karma, Metaphysics and Morals.

One is that the Vedantic Self-realisation and the understanding of the how and why of the World-process, *i.e.*, of the Relation between the Changeless Self (the "I") and the Changeful Not-Self (the "This"), is "some far-off divine event," "a mystic consecration and a dream," "a vision splendid like a lightning gleam," to be achieved in some far distant time and place, by the development of some special faculty of intuition, *bodhi, pratibha, divya-chakshu,* by some process of *yoga*, mysterious, unique, without a parallel in our everyday experience ; that the super-morals, or, indeed, superiority to all morals, which belong to such as have attained that realisation, are, or at least may be, very different in kind, from the morals that govern ordinary mortals ; and that Krishna's advic to Arjuna to "get beyond the three gunas" can have only an academicae ɪnterest for such.

The other view is that crossing "beyond the three *gunas*," becoming free of them, *nis-trai-gunya*, is just the realisation that the Self is "other than, opposite to, the Not-Self, the This," in which the "triple attributes" inhere ; that this realisation is possible here and now, and not a matter of any particular length of time and space;that the *yoga* needed is not different in *kind* from that exercised in every act of "attention," but only in *direction, i.e.*, it has to be not only extro-spective but also intro-spective (*Yoga-bhashya*, I, 1) [133] that "intellection" and "intuition" are the active and the passive, the ap-prehen-sive and the receptive, the (actively) focus-sive or selective and the (passively) re-flect-ive, the demarcative (delimitive, circum-scriptive) and the as-simil-ative, the *dharana* and the *dhyana-samadhi*, aspects or co-efficients of each other, being both included in

---

133 The *Gita* and the Upanishats too do not seem to mentiona ny faculty higher or subtler than the *buddhi*, though various adjectives are used to indicate that it must be refined and purified and perfected in order to see the Self (vi, 21 ; iii, 42 ; xviii, 20, 30, 51 in *Gita*; iii, 12 in *Katha*, etc.). *Sattviki, vishuddha, su-sukshma, agrya*, etc., are such adjectives. *Manisha, pratibha, prajna, bodhi*, seem to be only synonyms of perfected *buddhi*, purified, and *in-turned*, by *vairagya*, from clinging to the finite.

" attention," *yoga*—as first focussing and then receiving the imprint on the sensitive plate are both included in the one operation of photographing; that all Morals, for all stages and states of the soul, " bound " or " free," are fundamentally based on the facts and laws of Metaphysics (as Manu expressly says, vi, 82, and xii, 85—115), since the essence of Morals is nothing else than the mathematics of the permutations and combinations of just these six terms, *viz.*, selfishness, unselfishness, dutifulness (which in another aspect is Play-fulness), and pleasure, pain, peace (or, in another aspect, *Lila*-enjoyment) ; and that if and when a soul crosses beyond the three attributes of *sattva-rajas-tamas*,-[134] *i.e.*, realises the Negational Relation between the Self and the Not-Self, it no more becomes superior to morals, no more develops any code of super-morals, than it becomes superior to mathe matics or develops any super-mathematics which contradict and flout the elements of that science known to ordinary human beings. Selfishness, unselfishness, dutifulness also, and pleasure, pain, peace too, belong to the *upadhis*, the bodies, the dense and subtle sheaths of the Self, *i.e.*, to the pseudo-selves ; not to the Self Universal, to which belongs *Lila*, Play, in which all these are included equally. Selfishly give pain to another now, receive and suffer corresponding pain afterwards—this is *papa*, sin and its consequence; unselfishly give pleasure now, receive corresponding pleasure afterwards—this is *punya*, merit, and its consequence ; give pain or pleasure, as a matter of duty, without any personal feeling, in the spirit of an honest public servant, receive none afterwards, or receive them, if any, in corresponding spirit, dutifully—this is *naish-karmya*, duty, and its consequence ; Play-fully give pain or pleasure now, receive them Play-fully afterwards—this is *naish-karmya* and its consequence in another aspect, *Lila*. This seems to be the substance of the doctrine of *nis-trai-gunya* or *param-artha*, duty (or Play), as distinguished from *swartha*, " self-seeking," selfishness (or vice and sin), and *par-artha*, " other-seeking," unselfishness (or virtue and merit).

Such are the two views. They, at first sight, seem to contradict each other. Yet they are both true, and on Krishna's own authority, if any be needed. " One here and one there, out of millions, after many births and rebirths, understands (the) Me truly as being the All, the Whole," he says (*Gita*, vii, 3, 19). And yet he also says, and insistently, to Arjuna:

---

[134] For detailed discussion of the significance of these, see *The Science of Peace*, note at the end of ch. xi.

"Rise above the three *gunas*, become centred in the Self, become established in the Eternal, now, here, at once " (ii,45.) The reconciliation is simple. It is easily effected with the help of the metaphysical axiom that difference of standpoint makes difference of view ; difference of circumstance, difference of due.

The first view is true to the soul that occupies the position of,and holds the attitude corresponding to, the *arambha-vada* and the *bhakti-marga* ; the second, to the soul guided by the *advaita-vada* and the *jnana-marga* (see p. 106 *supra*).

It has been said before that, for the former, the *Aham* or I of the *Gita* means Krishna's great personality, and, for the latter, the Universal Self. So with the Christ's utterances : " I am the Way, the Truth, and the Life "; " I am the Light which lighteth every man who comes to this world"; " Without Me thou canst do nothing." To the former, I and Me mean Jesus ; to the latter, " (The) I am (=is) the Way (*Sat*), the Truth (*Chit*), and the Life (*Ananda*)," " (The) I am (=is) the only Light which (ultimately) lighteth every soul " ; " Without (the) Me thou canst do nothing." So with the saying of the prophets Isaiah and Muhammad : " There is no God other than (the) I."

Of its own wish, for " none-else compels," the soul turns its senses outwards, and pursues the "else," the objects of the senses. After traversing millions of cyclical years and billions of orbital miles on the winged globes of heaven (all matter of it-Self's own Supreme Imagination, Cosmic Ideation), it, again of its own wish, turns its senses inward, and then it sees at once that it is " None-Else than It-Self."

It is all a question of the *attitude* of the soul itself. " *Moksha* is not a change of conditions but of condition." Change of conditions, in the plural, may mean *siddhi-s*, extensions of faculty, other senses, greater powers, subtler bodies, all within the range of the finite. But that change of condition, in the singular, which means *moksha*, is just a change of the attitude of the soul towards itself, towards the world, towards the cause or substratum of both, *i.e.*, towards Man-Nature-God, Jiva-Jagad-Ishvara. Outward-turned, on the Path of Pursuit, Pravrtti, it thinks in terms of the first, second, and third persons, of I-You-He (-She-It), corresponding to Man-Nature-God, and they all remain separate ; God is a He, She, or It, and keeps distant from Man. Inward-turned, on the Path of Renunciation, Nivrtti, it thinks, in terms of the first person only, of I, and the separateness and the distance are annihilated, and God-Nature-Man all become One in " I-not-Another " (vii. 7). God is I, am I.

अस्ति ब्रह्मेति चेद्वेद परोक्षं ज्ञानमेव तत् ।
अस्मि ब्रह्मेति चेद्वेद अपरोक्षं तदुच्यते ॥

" Brahman *is*—is vicarious knowledge; Brahman *am*—is direct experience." As the Quran says : *Wa fi anfuse-kum a-fa-la tubserun*, " I am in you, but ye see Me not ".

A mystically-inclined western poet (Thompson) expresses a similar idea :

" The angels keep their ancient places,
Turn but a stone and start a wing ;
'Tis ye, 'tis you estranged faces,
That miss the many-splendoured Thing.
Does the fish soar to find the ocean,
The eagle plunge to find the air,
That we ask of the stars in motion
If they have rumour of Thee there ? "

The Sufis have said it more clearly :
" Dila ! tawaf-i-dilan kun
ke Kaaba-e-makhfi-st,
Ke an Khalil bina kard
wa in Khuda khud sakht."

*I.e.*,

Circumambulate thy-Self, O heart of mine !
Thou the true Kaaba, thou the holiest shrine !
That one Abraham builded of dead stone,
Thou wast built 'live by God's own hand divine !

And yet again more plainly, so plainly that the singer, Shams Tabrezi, was duly murdered and martyrised by the bigots whose souls he was trying, perhaps too insistently and prematurely, to illumine—though who knows but that the death helped to quicken, by reaction, the process of illumination :

" Ai qaum ba Haj rafta ! kuja-aid, kuja-aid !
Mashuq hamin ja-st, bi-ayaid, bi-ayaid !

Mashuq-i-to ham-saya-to, diwar ba diwar,
Dar badiya sar-gashta chi-ra-aid. chi-ra-aid !
Anan ki talabgar-i-Khuda aid, Khuda aid !
Hajat ba talab n-ist, shuma aid, shuma aid !
Chiz-e ke na gardid gum az bahr-i-chi joyaid ?
Kas ghair-i-shuma n-ist, chira-aid, chira-aid ! "

*I.e.,*

O pilgrims for the shrine ! where go ye, where !
Come back, come back, the Beloved is here !
His persence all your neighborhood doth bless !
Why will ye wander in the wilderness !
O ye that seek for God ! Yourselves are He !
There is no need to seek, He is ye, verily !
Why will ye seek for That which ne'er was lost ?
There is " None-Else-than-Ye " ! Be not doubt-tost !

So long as we keep our back to the sun we cannot see it, though eons pass ; when we turn our face to it we cannot help seeing it, that very instant. But the essential law of Nature. and therefore of Morals, remains the same. *after* the change of the soul's attitude as it was *before*, though the forms of the surroundings or of the relations between human beings (which relations are governed by that law) may change from time to time.

And that law is the law of action and reaction.

सुखस्यानंतरं दुःखं दुःखस्यानंतरं सुखम् ।

" After pleasure pain ; after pain, pleasure." They are always balancing up, in the long run or the short run. on all possible scales. *Punya* and *papa*, meritorious karma or sinful, chains of gold or chains of iron, pain first and pleasure afterwards or pleasure first and pain after—both have to be equal and opposite. lest the Repose of the Supreme be disturbed. The Zero, the Endless Circle, the Eternal Rest, the Absolute Equilibrium, the Universal Changeless Motionlessness, the Infinite Absence of all the Finites, necessitates, creates, imposes everywhere this law of the mutual abolition of pairedopposites by equal action and reaction. thereby providing at once for all possible Arbitrariness, Chance. Contingency, Disorder, Lawlessness of un-reason-ing Life-Desire, in the Nature of the World-process, and also for *pari passu* Obviation therof, by Lawful and Reasonable Negation.

As indicated in the *Gita*:

सर्वारंभा हि दोषेण धूमेनाग्निरिवावृता: । xviii, 48.
कर्मण्यकर्म य. पश्येदकर्मणि च कर्म यः ।
स बुद्धिमान् मनुष्येषु स युक्तः कृत्स्नकर्मकृत् ।। iv, 18.
यत्तदग्रे विषमिव परिणामेऽमृतोपमम् ।
परिणामे विषमिव यत्तदग्रेऽमृतोपमम् ।। xviii, 37,38.
नादत्ते कस्यचित्पापं न चैव सुकृतं विभुः । v, 15.
निर्मानमोहा जितसंगदोषा अध्यात्मनित्या विनिवृत्तकामा : ।
द्वंद्वैर्विमुक्ताः सुखदुःखसंज्ञैर्गच्छंत्यमूढाः पदमव्ययं तत् ।। xv, 5.
पुण्यं च पापं च पापे । (*Shariraka Bhashya*)

" There is no enterprise, no course of action, that does not involve both good and evil ; sin carries merit in its heart, merit sin ; he who realises this, he is wise, he performs all actions with equanimity, in the spirit of duty, he has done all there is to do ; that which is as venom at first is as nectar afterwards, and that which is as ambrosia to begin with is as poison in the end ; the Supreme Self is equally free of both ; (for both virtue and vice, merit and sin, are equally bonds, equally chains, though the one be of gold and the other of iron, even as creditor and debtor are both equally bound, to each other, by the loan, though the bond is pleasurable asset to the one and painful debt to the other ; and both belong to the pseudo-self, the *jiva*, the em-bodi-ed soul or the en-soul-ed body) ; and the soul that is tired of both pleasure and pain, and of all the countless pairs of opposites that are summed up in these two, gives up egoistic separateness and egoistic attachment, gives up clinging desire, accepts all befallings with resignation while doing its duties scrupulously, frees itself from the great Error of separate egoism from which all these arise, and rests peacefully in the Eternal."

When it is said that *dharmas*, morals, change from age to age (*Manu*, i, 85), differ for different persons (*Gita*, xviii, 41-46), are a matter of convention, what is meant is that a particular form of relationship between human beings with corresponding mutual rights-and-duties, which was found so long to yield more pleasure and less pain, on the whole, has, by gradual change of circumstances, and, usually, by the development of an *excess* (which, indeed, may be regarded as the prime sin) in one respect or another, begun to do the opposite, and so needs to be changed. But such variations need not, in any given case, of any individual or group of individuals, be regarded as constituting super-morals, but only as other forms of ordinary morals.

Thus, in respect of sex-relations and marriage—with which, and with property (essentially food, clothing, shelter, implements, etc.), as concerned with the fundamental problems of self-preservation and self-multiplicaion, morals are most intimately connected in human thought—the human race has tried scores of forms, all ranging between monogamy and promiscuity, and in respect of possessions, between nearly all separate property and nearly all common property ; and it is still experimenting, and will go on doing so, until the human body again changes its form, and hermaphrodite or a-sexual reproduction supervenes again, as in vegetable and protoz oic forms to-day,and,according to Puranic and Theosophical literature, in the very early human races, millions of years ago.

The *Smrtis* and the *Puranas*, in their descriptions of the various races of animals, men, rakshasas, devas, etc, mention dozens of types of matings and of progeny. The general principle underlying all changes seems to be always the same. All possible kinds of human marriages and domestic arrangements, as of economic, political,aesthetic, religious, etc., institutions and forms, are everlastingly present, in seed and potency, in the Human Sutratma, and each one of these is also connected more or less inseparably with all the others ; "all is everywhere and always" (*Gita*, xi, 40; xviii, 40) ; but only one set of forms, corresponding with each other, of the different yet connected aspects or departments of life, is manifested in any given time, place, and community. When the collective mass-mind (the particular Sutratma, of smaller or larger scale) of that community becomes surfeited with the experiences of that set of forms, and begins to take more pain than pleasure in them, then, after the inevitable struggle between its old desires and ways and the new, which manifests as a conflict between the conservatives and the radicals of that community, it makes a change, throws what was so far manifest into dormancy, and brings out into patency another set of forms which was up to now latent—comparatively.

Thus, one set of communist thinkers in Russia, and elsewhere, seem to have become dis-gusted with what they regard as the monotony of the too constant association, on the one hand, and, on the other, as the narrowing, selfish, clannish, emotions, of the family-life, as prevalent to-day, and its incidents of private, exclusive, heritable and iniquitously distributed property ; and they want wider, larger, more extensive emotions, which are, according to them, the concomitants of only freedom in sex-relations and in property. " . . . With constancy of contact . . . passion dims and love fades into indifference, dislike, or devotion. The exhilaration which we have called romance is irretrievably lost. . . The disappearance of bourgeois monogamy will remove these family restrictions, and open up the possibilities for the growth of the social emotions in a more communal life. Men and women will have affections that will become expansive and not ingrown. Sorrows will not be limited to a small group, nor pleasures shared in clannish form. Social sympathy will supersede family avarice " : (Calverton, *The Bankruptcy of Marriage*, pp. 280-282 ; pub. 1929). And they are therefore proposing, side by side with the abolition of private property, what seems, in effect, to be, a reversion, on a more intelligent and higher level, in a regulated form, to the free unions of some primitive human tribes, or of the so-called higher animals, or, better, of the gods and nymphs, *gandharva-s* and *apsara-s*, in *Swarga* (heaven). This is said without any sarcasm, or prejudiced implication of condemnation : for animals, and primitive or non-primitive men, and gods and goddesses, all are equally manifestations of the Supreme ; and we must all " live and let live ". But just to ensure this last, of letting live mutually, and in so far as pros and cons have to be discussed before a course of action can be settled on among persons who are to live and work together, it may be pointed out that the denizens of heaven have been " cursed " by Parvati (according to the Puranas, though some extremists in birth-control might well say " blessed ") with complete sterility, and deprivation of the " love of children " (which however might be regarded by some as amply compensated for by freedom from responsibility and " worry ") ; that the *Kalpa-taru*, the " Wishing-Tree " (of Imagination), which stands in the middle of the public Pleasure-Park of Swarga, called Nandana (the Joyful Paradise—of mind), gives to each of them all desired bliss-dreams only so long as his or her bank-account of *punya*-merit lasts ; and that when it is exhausted, he or she is flung down ruthlessly into this lower world again to earn " merit "-cash anew—all which seems to have meaning, and a meaning not altogether useless for or inapplicable to mundane human affairs. In any and every case, the metaphysical axiom holds true that error lies in the extremes. and truth and right in the mean (*Gita*, vi, 16-17). In trying to avoid Scylla we must not rush into the maw of Charybdis ; if excessive individualism or familism is the devil, excessive socialism or communism is the deep sea. We want " I " and " we " both. We cannot understand, we cannot feel, either without the other. If we try to abolish either, we will abolish the other too. It we cut away the individual-tree-groups, we will not have any communal-wood left. Those who cannot get on with members of their family, stand its discipline, learn to bear and forbear,are not likely to be able to get on with their community, except as parasites. What is needed is a rational humanism which will avoid excesses on either side and will balance and synthesise the individualist and the communist aspects of life, both equally indispensable—always remembering, that no scheme can abolish evil and pain altogether, that the best scheme is that which minimises these in any given set of circumstances, and that this minimisation is possible only when the facts and the laws of the psychology and the physiology of individuals and groups is duly taken into account, and the exhilaration of short-lived passionate romance, very valuable experience though it be, is yet regarded, not as an end in itself, but as a means of kindling permanent steady spiritual affection and devotion, towards the members of the family, thence towards kith and kin, thence towards fellow-beings, generally, and finally towards the Self in all. The relationship of Purusha and Prakrti, of husband and wife, includes all relationships, of spouse and spouse, brother and sister, father and daughter, mother and son. friend and friend, of equal and at the same time younger as well as elder. Husband and wife are all these to each other, as is expressly declared by Dasharatha with reference to Kausalya (*Ramayana*. Aranya. ch. 12), and by Shakuntala to Dushyanta (*Mbh.*, Adi-parva, ch. 98). All these relationships obviously spring out of, and are therefore always included in, the primal relationship of man and woman, which finds its fulfilment, its complete manifestation, only in and through all these. only when all these are duly and fully developed. It is only the abiding spiritual affections belonging to these which can make it possible that "joy becomes duty and love becomes law." They whd wish to avoid these. and to taste only the passions and sensations ano exhilarations of "romance," seem to be like persons who wish to live wholly on spices and wines,without any really nourishing substantial food at all. They will, in all probability, fall very ill psychically or physically or both very soon—so psychology and physiology seem to indicate. The family, and not the individual, is the unit of the community (*Manu*, ix, 45). The community grows out of the family, is an expansion of the family, as a forest is of groups of different kinds of trees, and is meaningless without it. Communal life, social emotions, social pleasures and sorrows and sympathies, are only copies and dilutions of those of the family, and are as difficult to feel without having first felt the latter, as it is to understand the rule of three without having mastered the mysteries of addition and subtraction. To belittle, to weaken, to destroy the family is to lay the axe at the root of the community also. If "famili-arity breeds contempt" in those who do not know how to avoid excess, they will find that "commun-ality breeds disgust" even more quickly. It is quite likely that the revels of the West (see p. 157 *supra*) are the reaction from, and the rewards of, and are therefore exhausting, the spiritual forces stored up by the self-denial, the *tapas*, of the emigrant Puritan ancestors, which forces have built up the greatness of the U.S.A.; even as Ravana's excessive self-indulgence exhausted his *tapas*-merit and destroyed him and his empire.

We may admire greatly the poetry of sound in singing *gandharva-s* (the musicians of heaven), and the poetry of motion in *apsara-s* (celestial dancers), but our whole-hearted worship is given to Gauri-Shankara, *Ardha-nar-ishwara*, the divinity who is both man and woman at once. Not equality, which means perpetual odious comparison, and thence conflict, but "identity of man and woman and child," in head, in heart, in interests, in the family—this is the basis of the happy and prosperous community; so declares Manu (ix, 45), and he does not allow any double standard of morality, but enjoins pre-marital virginity and post-marital chastity for both man and woman equally.

Therefore does reverent salutation well up from the Indian heart, for the Mother, *Vande Mataram* : not for man or woman as man or woman, but for the woman as *Mother* (*Manu*. ii, 145), the preserver of life, generation after generation.

Therefore have all the great Teachers done homage to the Family unanimously. Krishna can find no higher words than the terms of the Family by which to describe the Supreme (see pp. 100-102 *supra*) : "I am the Father, the Mother, the Spouse, the Friend, the Home and Refuge." Jesus says (Matthew, 19) : "Honor thy father and mother (and teacher) and love thy (spouse and child and) neighbor as thy-Self. Thou shalt do no murder ; thou shalt commit no adultery ; thou shalt not steal ; thou shalt not bear false witness ; thou shalt (not amass riches for thyself, but) give to the poor." The Budhha says almost exactly the same in the "Mahamangala Sutta" and the "Pancha-shila". The Puranas and the *Yoga-sutras* (ii, 30) repeat the words. And Manu, first and foremost of them all enjoins the very same (x. 63 ; ii. 226-232 ; iv, 182-185). Muhammad the prophet says : *Al jannato tahata qadam-ilumm*, "heaven spreads beneath the feet of mothers".

Respect for the relationships of the family, and for its righteous and not excessive possessions, has thus, generally, always formed the skeletal system of all codes of morals, though the details have differed. This is inevitable, since they are psycho-physically connected with the development of the individual consciousness and sex-difference and the three physical and the three psychical *eshanas* or appetites. [135]

So long and so far as human beings have the sense of separate individuality, so long and so far they will suffer, and will fear, pain and death. And so long and so far as they suffer and fear pain and death, they must and will have the regulations and the consolations of Law, Morals, Religion, Philosophy, in crude or refined form, according to their stage of evolution. The soul that has realised, has become assured of, its immortality, as identical with the Supreme Spirit in essence, has risen, as Spirit, not as body, beyond the regions of the mortal, wherein the *gunas*, the triple attributes, aspects, functions, (cognition-desire-action and quality-substance-movement) of mind-matter reign. It has therefore automatically risen above all Law, Morals, Religion, Philosophy; [136] yet *not* that it can now flout and violate

---

[135] See *The Science of the Emotions*, ch. III (B).

[136] A western poet, Chapman, has caught the idea well, but it is difficult to say whether with its full and proper implications :

> "There is no danger to a man that knows
> What life and death is ; there's not any law
> Exceeds his knowledge ; neither is it lawful
> That he should stoop to any other law."

Cf. The familiar Sanskrit verse, निस्त्रैगुण्ये पथि विचरतो को विधिः निषेधः, को often misapplied by the vicious, in the way in which "the devil can quote Scripture for his purpose".

them, but that it may help to uphold the essentials of them the more strongly ; since it has become identified with the very fount and source of them, Dharma-megha, Atma-Buddhi (see p. 135, *supra*); though it may help to change the outer forms and expressions of them, the non-essential details, from time to time, as necessary. Krishna expressly forbids all self-deceiving and other-misleading assumption of " superiority to morals " by the wise soul " which has seen and known the All " (*Gita*, iii, 19-29).

If such a soul should " transgress," in any of its bodies, any law of God's Nature and Nature's God, *i.e.*, of the Supreme Spirit which is it-Self, then it would be, and it would know all the while that it would surely and rightly be, " punished " also, in corresponding bodies. The case of Ravana, as such transgressor, and in very flagrantly evil degree, despite knowledge, is well-known in Indian legend. The expiation of their gentler, more refined, and even sometimes amiable errings, by Avataras, has been referred to before (see pp. 16-58-61, *supra*). We are told that the Buddha and other *ishwarajivas*, " lordly self-governing souls," are reaping the consequences, glorious from one standpoint, painful from another, of excessive compassion. 137 We may close with another instance, which will perhaps help to illustrate whatever distinction, without difference, may be at all possible to draw, for purposes of technical terminology, between morals and super-morals.

---

137 The theosophical version is that, because of excessive compassion, Gautama Buddha overdid his part in the Great Plan of Human Evolution and made public some portions of the Secret Wisdom prematurely. To remedy the disturbance caused thereby, he has to remain in touch with the Humanity of this Earth, and cannot pass away wholly to other spheres, of work and rest, as he might have done otherwise ; and he appears as a glorious image in the sky, over a certain spot in Thibet, on the full-moon night of every Vaishakha (see p. 134 *supra*). The exoteric Buddhist works say that his favorite disciple, Ananda, was so inconsolable when Buddha was giving up his body that he promised to keep in touch for a *kalpa*. The corresponding Puranic tradition is that Shuka, the son of Vyasa, passed into *videha mukti* and dissolved into space and disappeared, at the age of twelve years, even as Vyasa was looking at him ; and that when the distracted father tried to pursue him and bring him back, and would not be persuaded to desist in any other way, then his recent son created, out

After the Great War, Yudhishthira, trembling with mixed emotions, goes, with Krishna, to wait upon his uncle and his aunt, the blind king Dhrtarashtra and the queen Gandhari, all whose sons, headed by Duryodhana, have been slain by Bhima, in the War. Gandhari is overpowered by grief and wrath, and falls down, and cries out upon Krishna : "You had the power to prevent this slaughter. You did not. I pronounce this doom on you that your own kith and kin shall perish too by internecine slaughter, and yourself shall come to a nameless end." Then Krishna smiling slightly and sadly : "You are failing still to let your soul be chastened by your sorrows. You are failing still to recognise that they have been brought on you by yourself. Why did you not throw all your weight on my side when I did all that was right to do to dissuade your son Duryodhana from his evil purpose ? To save yourself from further evil deed and sorrow, I am utilising your long-gathered *tapas*-force now turned to rage. By my own wish you are foretelling, and helping with your wrathful will, that which is the last scene in the drama planned out by myself. That scene will take place thirty-six years hence. None may destroy this body of mine against my wish. So I will bring it to a nameless end, for many reasons. None may destroy the Yadavas, my kith and kin in this life, but themselves. So they will pass, also, as warriors should, by each other's hands, after having played their part and done their work on earth, for the further progress of the Human Race.

---

of his bodiless being, a *chhaya-Shuka*, a "shadow-image of Shuka," which came and lived with Vyasa for his consolation. Theosophical literature speaks of "living" astral images, and also of Buddha being an incarnation of Vyasa. The *Bhagavata* says that the rshi Maitreya (also called Kausharavi, because his mother was Mitra and his father Kusharava) was a very dear friend of Vyasa as Ananda (Maitreya Bodhisattva) of the Buddha; and one Theosophical belief is that Vyasa reincarnated as the Buddha.

# INDEX

(OF WORKS REFERRED TO)

# INDEX

OF SUFI ARABIC-PERSIAN WORDS

*(Samskrt equivalents and explanations in English will be found on the pages mentioned)*